NuWave Oven Cookbook

NuWave Oven Cookbook

The Complete Guide to Making the Most of Your NuWave Oven

Copyright © 2017 by Dylanna Press
All rights reserved. This book or any portion thereof
may not be reproduced or used in any manner whatsoever without the express written permission of the
publisher except for the use of brief quotations in a book review.

First edition: 2017

Disclaimer/Limit of Liability
This book is for informational purposes only. The views expressed are those of the author alone, and should not be taken as expert, legal, or medical advice. The reader is responsible for his or her own actions.
Every attempt has been made to verify the accuracy of the information in this publication. However, neither the author nor the publisher assumes any responsibility for errors, omissions, or contrary interpretation of the material contained herein.
This book is not intended to provide medical advice. Please see your health care professional before embarking on any new diet or exercise program. The reader should regularly consult a physician in matters relating to his/her health and particularly with respect to any symptoms that may require diagnosis or medical attention.
This book is not endorsed by or affiliated with the NuWave Oven corporation. All trademarks are property of their respective owners.

Photo credits: Shutterstock

Contents

Advantages of Cooking with the NuWave Oven 1

Science of NuWave Ovens 2

NuWave Ovens versus Halogen Ovens 2

Tips and Tricks for Cooking with the NuWave Oven 2

Frequently Asked Questions 3

NuWave Oven Temperature Conversion Guide 4

Breakfast and Egg Dishes 5

Appetizers and Sandwiches 23

Poultry 39

Pork 75

Beef and Lamb 97

Seafood 113

Vegetables and Side Dishes 141

Desserts and Baked Goods 171

From the Author 197

Index 199

More Bestselling Titles from Dylanna Press 205

1

WHETHER YOU'RE NEW to the world of infrared ovens or have been using a NuWave Oven for years, the *NuWave Oven Cookbook: The Complete Guide to Getting the Most Out of Your NuWave Oven* is going to help you make amazingly healthy and delicious meals that you and your family and friends are going to love.

Many people are excited when they first purchase a NuWave Oven but aren't really sure what to do with it. While the NuWave Oven is great for roasting chicken and other meats, it has the potential to be used for so much more.

This book contains a plethora of recipes that can all be made quickly and easily right in your NuWave Oven. So what are you waiting for?

Happy cooking!

Advantages of Cooking with the NuWave Oven

The NuWave Oven makes cooking fast, easy, and convenient. With the NuWave Oven you can do so much – including baking, grilling, broiling, steaming, and roasting. The NuWave Oven will save you time, cooking foods faster, even allowing you to cook foods to perfection directly from frozen, so if you forget to take something out of the freezer for dinner, don't despair!

Other advantages of the NuWave Oven include:

- **Energy efficient** – uses 85% less energy than traditional cooking methods
- **Fast** – cooks up to 50% faster than traditional cooking methods
- **Portable** – weighing only about 9 pounds, you can easily take your oven with you wherever you need it
- **Safe** – no smoke, no flame
- **Healthy** – seals in juices, fat drips away
- **Convenient** – cook straight from frozen, no need to defrost
- **Time saving** – no need to preheat
- **Multiple uses** – broil, roast, grill, bake, barbecue
- **Advanced technology** – combines conduction, convection, and infrared heat
- **Easy to clean** – dishwasher safe, put everything except for the power head right in the dishwasher

The NuWave Oven has so many advantages that you will find yourself wondering how you ever lived without it. In fact, many people say they cook with it every day and rarely use their conventional oven anymore.

Science of NuWave Ovens

NuWave Ovens use a combination of three different heating methods to cook food. It combines conduction, convention, and infrared heat.

- **Conduction** – This is a type of heat that is applied directly to food.
- **Convection** – This heating method circulates hot air throughout the oven using a fan. It allows for even distribution of heat and faster cooking times.
- **Infrared heat** – This is a type of heat energy that penetrates food, allowing the food to cook from both the inside and the outside at the same time. It helps to lock in flavor and juices.

By combining all three of these technologies, the NuWave Oven provides a superior method of cooking, allowing you to bake, broil, grill, and air-fry in record time, without sacrificing taste. In fact, most people find the foods they cook in the NuWave Oven are superior in quality to those in a traditional oven.

NuWave Ovens versus Halogen Ovens

Typical halogen ovens use a halogen bulb as a heating source. These provide only 1200 watts of energy and require regular replacement. The NuWave Oven uses a 1500-watt Sheath Heater that will last up to 30 years without needing to be replaced.

The NuWave Oven comes with several safety features that give it an advantage over the typical halogen oven. First, NuWave Ovens feature a patented locking mechanism that secures the dome cover in place and prevents steam from escaping. Second, NuWave Ovens use a lighter, break-resistant plastic dome unlike the glass domes of most halogen ovens. This is an advantage because in addition to not shattering like glass if accidently dropped, the plastic dome is also cooler than the glass domes, which can get very hot during cooking, potentially causing burns.

NuWave Ovens, due to their unique combination of conduction, convection, and infrared technology, provide much more even cooking than halogen ovens. Halogen ovens can cook food unevenly, resulting in dishes that are partially undercooked and partially burnt.

Tips and Tricks for Cooking with the NuWave Oven

To help you get the most out of your NuWave Oven, we offer these tips and tricks.

- When cooking different types of food at the same time, place those requiring the longest cooking time on the rack closest to the heating element. Place faster cooking items below on lower rack.
- Unless recipe instructs otherwise, promptly remove food from NuWave Oven when

cooking is complete. Steam and moisture can build up under the dome and cause food to become soggy. This can be avoided by removing cooked items once cooking has completed.
- To season meat, chicken, or fish when cooking from frozen, first sprinkle food with water and then add seasoning. This will help the seasonings to be absorbed.
- Oven cooking times can vary considerably, depending on size of food and other factors. It is always best to test for doneness using a meat thermometer. See the internal meat temperature guide for recommended temperatures.
- To steam food, sprinkle with water before placing in NuWave Oven.
- When dehydrating it is important that you remove food immediately when cooking is complete in order to avoid sogginess.
- To ensure even cooking, most foods will need to be flipped about halfway through cooking time.
- Remember, the heating element is at the top of the oven. Therefore, to broil or grill, place food on the higher rack. To roast, place on lower rack.
- Tips for converting recipes
  o If the recipe directions call for temperatures above 350°F, then cook for the same time stated in the directions.
  o If the recipe directions call for temperatures below 350°F, then cook for 25% less time than stated in the directions.

Frequently Asked Questions

What type of cookware can be used in the NuWave Oven?
Any cookware that can be used in a conventional oven can also be used in a NuWave Oven. Metal, glass, and silicone cookware are all safe for use in the oven, as well as foil and oven-safe cooking bags.

What is the 3-inch Extender Ring used for?
The Extender Ring is used for cooking larger-sized items such as a turkey or ham. It can also be used for multi-level cooking.

How can the NuWave Oven be cleaned?
One of the advantages of using the NuWave Oven is the ease of cleanup. All parts, with the exception of the Power Head, are dishwasher safe. However, to protect the surfaces, do not use abrasive cleaners or scouring pads. Always turn off and unplug oven before cleaning.

Does the NuWave Oven need to be ventilated?
The NuWave Oven produces less heat than a conventional oven and produces little to no smoke. Ventilation is typically not needed.

What are the different racks in the NuWave Oven?
The standard rack can be used as both a 1-inch rack or as a 4-inch rack when flipped. Some models also include either a 2-inch rack or a 3-inch rack. By using and/or stacking different rack heights, multiple foods can be cooked at the same time.

NuWave Oven Temperature Conversion Guide

Power Level	Oven Temperature
10 (HI)	342°F (172°C)
9	325°F (163°C)
8	300°F (149°C)
7	275°F (135°C)
6	250°F (121°C)
5	225°F (107°C)
4	175°F (79°C)
3	150°F (66°C)
2	116°F (47°C)
1	106°F (41°C)

2
Breakfast and Egg Dishes

Start your day off right with a healthy and delicious breakfast.

BACON

Cooking bacon in the NuWave Oven is easy and turns out delicious!

Servings: 4-6

10-12 slices bacon

1. Line bottom of oven with foil to catch bacon grease.
2. Place bacon slices on 4-inch rack.
3. Cook on High power (350 degrees F) for 8 minutes. Flip bacon over and cook for an additional 5 minutes or until bacon reaches desired crispness.

EGG AND BACON BREAKFAST MUFFINS

These muffins make an easy breakfast to take on the go.
Servings: 6

5 eggs
½ cup bacon crumbles
¼ cup chopped onion
¼ cup chopped red bell pepper
4 tablespoons milk
Sea salt and ground black pepper, to taste
¼ shredded cheddar cheese

1. Spray 6 cup muffin pan with cooking spray.
2. Beats eggs in large bowl. Stir in bacon crumbles, onion, bell pepper, salt, and pepper. Fold in grated cheese.
3. Spoon mixture into muffin cups.
4. Place muffin pan on 1-inch rack. Cook on High Power (350 degrees F) for 15-20 minutes, until knife inserted in center of muffin comes out clean.

HEALTHY LOW-FAT GRANOLA

Store-bought granola can be high in sodium and fat. Making your own is easy in your NuWave Oven! Whip up a batch and store it for up to a week.

Servings: 8

- 4 cups old-fashioned oats
- 1/4 cup flax seed
- 1/4 cup wheat germ
- 1/4 cup coconut flakes
- 1/4 cup pumpkin or sunflower seeds
- 1/4 sliced almonds
- 1/3 cup maple syrup
- 1/4 cup apple juice
- 1 teaspoon cinnamon
- 1 teaspoon vanilla
- 1/4 teaspoon salt

1. In a large bowl, combine all ingredients. Stir well to thoroughly coat all ingredients.
2. Line rimmed cookie sheet with parchment paper. Spread mixture evenly on cookie sheet.
3. Place pan in NuWave on 1-inch rack. Cook at 350 degrees at power level high for 10 minutes. Stir, and cook for an addition 10-15 minutes, until lightly browned.

BAKED GREEK OMELET WITH TOMATOES AND FETA

This colorful omelet makes a wonderful breakfast or light lunch.
Servings: 4

8 eggs
¼ cup milk
½ cup fresh baby spinach, chopped
2 green onions, sliced
1 teaspoon dried oregano
¾ cup feta cheese, crumbled
12-15 grape tomatoes, halved
12-15 Kalamata olives, chopped
Sea salt and freshly ground black pepper, to taste

1. In a medium size bowl, whisk together the eggs and milk until fluffy. Stir in spinach, green onions, oregano, feta cheese, tomatoes, and olives. Season with salt and pepper.
2. Pour into 8 x 8 baking dish.
3. Bake on 1-inch rack on High power (350 degrees F) for 13-15 minutes. Let sit for an additional minute or two before serving.

BAKED EGGS WITH SPINACH AND TOMATOES

This impressive breakfast or brunch dish is actually very easy to make.
Servings: 4

8 ounces frozen spinach, chopped, thawed

3 medium plum tomatoes, chopped

¼ teaspoon garlic powder

¼ teaspoon red pepper flakes

Sea salt and freshly ground black pepper, to taste

8 large eggs

2 tablespoons cream

½ cup shredded cheddar cheese

1. Spray 8 x 8 casserole dish with cooking spray.
2. Squeeze out excess moisture from thawed spinach.
3. Spread tomatoes on bottom of casserole dish. Layer spinach on top of tomatoes. Season with garlic powder, red pepper flakes, salt, and pepper. Crack eggs on top, drizzle with cream, and sprinkle with cheese.
4. Place dish on 1-inch rack. Bake on High power (350 degrees F) for 15 minutes or until egg whites are opaque.

HAM, CHEESE, AND BACON QUICHE

Makes and excellent brunch or light dinner.
Servings: 8

1 9-inch pie crust
1 cup ham, diced
4 slices bacon, cooked and crumbled
1 ½ cups shredded cheddar cheese
1 tablespoon flour
3 eggs
1 ½ cups milk
Sea salt and freshly ground black pepper, to taste

1. Place pie crust on 1-inch rack and bake on High power (350 degrees) for 6-7 minutes, until just starting to brown. Remove from oven and allow to cool.
2. Spread ham and bacon evenly across bottom of pie crust. Sprinkle cheese evenly on top.
3. In bowl, mix together flour, eggs, milk, salt, and pepper. Pour mixture into pie crust.
4. Place on 1-inch rack and bake on High power (350 degrees F) for 15 minutes. Reduce heat to Power Level 8 (300 degrees F) and cook for an additional 10 minutes or until toothpick inserted in center comes out clean. Let quiche sit for 10 minutes before slicing.

SPRING FRITTATA WITH SMOKED SALMON AND ASPARAGUS

Servings: 4

8 eggs
½ cup milk
¾ teaspoon salt
¼ teaspoon black pepper
1 cup cooked asparagus, chopped
4 ounces smoked salmon, chopped
¼ cup chives, chopped
¼ cup flat-leaf parsley, chopped

1. In large bowl, whisk together eggs and milk. Season with salt and pepper. Fold in asparagus, salmon, chives, and parsley.
2. Pour egg mixture into liner pan. Bake on High power (350 degrees F) for 35 to 40 minutes, or until toothpick in center comes out clean. If top starts to get too brown, cover with foil during last part of cooking.
3. Serve frittata immediately or allow to cool to room temperature. May also be refrigerated for up to 1 day and served cold.

SUN-DRIED TOMATO AND GOAT CHEESE FRITTATA WITH BASIL

Makes a quick and easy breakfast or brunch dish.
Servings: 4

1 tablespoon olive oil

1 medium yellow onion, chopped small

8 eggs

½ cup milk

½ teaspoon salt

¼ teaspoon ground pepper

6 ounces sun-dried tomatoes, chopped

½ cup goat cheese

½ cup basil, chopped

1. Heat olive oil in pan over medium heat and sauté onions until translucent, 3-4 minutes.
2. In large bowl, whisk together eggs and milk. Season with salt and pepper. Fold in sun-dried tomatoes, goat cheese, and basil, and onion.
3. Pour egg mixture into liner pan. Bake on High power (350 degrees F) for 35 to 40 minutes, or until toothpick in center comes out clean. If top starts to get too brown, cover with foil during last part of cooking.
4. Serve frittata immediately or allow to cool to room temperature. May also be refrigerated for up to 1 day and served cold.

OVERNIGHT BAKED BLUEBERRY AND CREAM CHEESE FRENCH TOAST

Make this when you want a special treat.
Servings: 4

Cooking spray
8 slices thick-cut bread (French or sourdough), day old is best, cut into 1-inch cubes
8 ounces cream cheese, cut into cubes
1 cup fresh or frozen blueberries
6 eggs
1 cup milk
½ teaspoon vanilla extract
½ teaspoon cinnamon
¼ cup maple syrup
1/3 cup flour
1/3 cup brown sugar, packed
¼ teaspoon cinnamon
4 tablespoons butter, cubed

1. Spray 8x8-inch baking pan with cooking spray. Layer half off the bread cubes in the bottom of pan. Layer half of bread cubes on bottom of pan. Add layer of cream cheese cubes and ½ of blueberries, spreading evenly over bread.
2. In bowl, whisk together eggs, milk, vanilla extract, cinnamon, and maple syrup. Pour over bread cubes.
3. In bowl, mix together flour, brown sugar, and cinnamon. Cut in butter, mixing with fork or fingers, until mixture is crumbly. Spread over bread cubes. Top with remaining blueberries.
4. Cover with foil and place in refrigerator overnight or a minimum of 2-3 hours.
Place baking dish on 1-inch rack and cook on High power (350 degrees F) for 30 minutes.
5. Top with additional blueberries and whipped cream, if desired.

CRAB QUICHE

Servings: 8

1 9-inch pie crust

4 eggs

1 cup heavy cream or half and half

Sea salt and freshly ground black pepper, to taste

1 teaspoon hot sauce (or more to taste)

1 cup Monterey Jack cheese, shredded

¼ cup grated Parmesan cheese

1 green onion, chopped

2 cans lump crabmeat

1. Place pie crust on 1-inch rack and bake on High power (350 degrees) for 6-7 minutes, until just starting to brown. Remove from oven and allow to cool.
2. In a large bowl, mix together eggs, cream, salt, pepper, and hot sauce. Stir in cheeses, onion, and crabmeat. Pour into pie crust.
3. Place on 1-inch rank and bake on power level High (350 degrees F) for 15 minutes. Reduce heat to Power level 8 (300 degrees F) and cook for an additional 10-15 minutes or until toothpick inserted in center comes out clean. Allow to sit for 10 minutes before serving.

3
Appetizers and Sandwiches

The NuWave Oven makes delicious sandwiches as well as starters.

AVOCADO WRAPPED IN BACON

Creamy on the inside and crispy on the outside. Delicious!
Servings: 10 appetizers

1 avocado
10 slices bacon

1. Cut avocado in half and remove pit.
2. Slice each avocado lengthwise into 5 pieces per side. Remove from skin.
3. Wrap each avocado slice in piece of bacon.
4. Place on 4-inch rack.
5. Cook on High power (350 degrees F) for 8 minutes. Turn over and cook for an additional 5 minutes.

ASPARAGUS WRAPPED IN BACON

Servings: 4

1 bunch asparagus (about 1 ½ pounds), ends trimmed
2 tablespoons extra-virgin olive oil
Salt and freshly ground black pepper, to taste
4 slices bacon
Lemon wedges for serving

1. Drizzle olive oil over asparagus spears to lightly coat. Season with salt and pepper.
2. Divide asparagus spears into 4 bundles. Wrap a slice of bacon securely around each bundle.
3. Arrange asparagus bundles on 4-inch rack. Bake on High power (350 degrees F) for 15-18 minutes, turning once, until bacon is crisp and asparagus is tender. Serve with lemon wedges.

SWEET AND SPICED NUTS

These are great to serve at a party.
Servings: 12

1 cup walnut halves
1 cup pecan halves
1 cup cashews
1 cup almonds
3 tablespoons butter, melted
½ cup white sugar
¼ cup water
½ teaspoon cumin
½ teaspoon cayenne pepper
1 teaspoon salt
½ teaspoon ground pepper

1. Combine walnuts, pecans, cashews, and almonds in large bowl.
2. in small bowl melted butter, sugar, water, cumin, cayenne pepper, salt, and pepper. Pour mixture over nuts. Stir to coat nuts thoroughly.
3. Spread nuts in liner pan. Cook on power level High (350 degrees F) for 10 minutes. Stir and cook for an additional 3-4 minutes.

BACON-WRAPPED JALAPENO POPPERS

Servings: 18 poppers

8 ounces cream cheese, softened
1/3 cup cheddar cheese, shredded
9 jalapeno peppers, halved lengthwise, deseeded
9 slices bacon, thin cut, cut in half

1. In a bowl, mix together cream cheese and cheddar cheese until blended.
2. Fill each jalapeno half with cheese mixture.
3. Wrap each stuffed pepper with slice of bacon.
4. Arrange peppers on foil-lined baking sheet.
5. Place baking sheet on 4-inch rack. Cook on High power (350 degrees F) for 12-15 minutes until bacon is crispy.

SPINACH AND SUN-DRIED TOMATO STUFFED MUSHROOMS

These bold-flavored mushrooms make an excellent starter.

Servings: 12-15 mushrooms

½ pound baby Portobello mushrooms (about 12-15 mushrooms)
Sea salt and freshly ground black pepper, to taste 2 tablespoons olive oil
2 cloves garlic, minced
¾ cup baby spinach, chopped
1/3 cup sun-dried tomatoes, chopped
½ cup Asiago cheese, grated

1. Wash and remove stems from mushrooms. Coat shallow baking dish with cooking spray. Arrange mushrooms in pan. Season with salt and pepper.
2. Heat olive oil in skillet over medium-high heat. Add garlic, sauté for 1-2 minutes, add spinach and cook until wilted. Remove pan from heat. Add sun-dried tomatoes, season with salt and pepper, and mix well.
3. Fill each mushroom cap with spinach and sun-dried tomato mixture. Top with asiago cheese.
4. Place on 3-inch rack and cook on High power (350 degrees F) for 5-6 minutes or until mushroom are tender and cheese is bubbly.

OPEN-FACED TUNA MELT

Quick and delicious, this makes a great lunch or even a light dinner.

Servings: 2

1 can Albacore tuna, drained
1 tablespoon capers
1 tablespoon chives, chopped
1 teaspoon dried basil
Sea salt and freshly ground black pepper, to taste
2 tablespoons mayonnaise
2 slices sour dough or multigrain bread
4 tomato slices
¼ shredded cheddar cheese
4 slices avocado

1. In a bowl, combine tuna, capers, chives, basil, salt, pepper, and mayonnaise. Mix until well combined.
2. Place bread slices on 3-inch rack. Cook on High power (350 degrees F) for 2-3 minutes until bread is light golden brown.
3. Remove toast from oven and divide tuna mixture evenly between the slices. Top each slice with two tomato slices and shredded cheese. Return to 3-inch rack and cook on High power for an additional 2-3 minutes, or until cheese is golden brown.
4. Top with avocado and additional salt and pepper.

ARTICHOKE GRILLED CHEESE SANDWICH

If you like artichoke dip then you are going to love this sandwich.

Servings: 2

4 ounces cream cheese, softened

1/3 cup mayonnaise

½ cup shredded cheddar cheese

½ shredded Mozzarella cheese

½ teaspoon garlic salt

1 7-ounce jar of artichoke hearts, chopped

4 slices French bread, about ½-inch thick

Butter, for spreading on bread

1. In a bowl, cream together cream cheese and mayonnaise until smooth. Stir in cheddar cheese, Mozzarella cheese, garlic salt, and artichokes.
2. Butter one side of each slice of bread. Place two slices of bread, buttered side down on 3-inch rack. Spread ½ of cheese mixture onto each slice. Top with another slice of bread, buttered side up.
3. Cook on High power (350 degrees F) for 3 minutes. Flip over and cook for an additional 3 minutes until cheese is melted and bread is golden.

GRILLED CHEESE WITH AVOCADO AND TOMATO

Another take on the classic grilled cheese.
Servings: 2

4 slices sourdough bread
Butter, for spreading on bread
8 ounces gruyere cheese, sliced
1 tomato, sliced
1 avocado, peeled, pitted, and sliced
1 tomato, sliced
Sea salt and ground black pepper, to taste

1. Butter one side of each slice of bread. Place two slices of bread, buttered side down, on 3-inch rack.
2. Layer each slice of bread with sliced of cheese, tomato, and avocado. Season with salt and pepper. Top with another side of bread, buttered side up.
3. Grill on Power Level High (350 degrees F) for 3-4 minutes. Turn over and cook for an additional 3-4 minutes.

4
Poultry

There are so many ways to cook chicken and turkey in the NuWave Oven and all of them are delicious!

MEDITERRANEAN LEMON CHICKEN AND POTATOES

Servings: 2

3/4 pound chicken breast, skinless and boneless, cut into 1-inch cubes
1/2 pound Yukon Gold potatoes, cut into cubes
1/2 medium onion, chopped
1/2 red or yellow pepper, chopped
1/4 cup low-sodium vinaigrette
1/8 cup lemon juice
1/2 teaspoon oregano
1/4 teaspoon garlic powder
1/4 cup chopped tomato
Freshly ground black pepper, to taste

1. Mix all ingredients except tomatoes together in large bowl.
2. Lay out 2 large squares of aluminum foil. Place equal amount of chicken and potato mixture in the center of each square. Fold top and sides to enclose mixture in packet.
3. Place packets on 3-inch rack and cook at 350 degrees (High) for 11-13 minutes or until chicken and potatoes are cooked through. (Add additional 2-3 minutes of cooking time if cooking chicken from frozen.)
4. Open packets and top with chopped tomatoes. Season with black pepper to taste.

CREAMY CHICKEN AND CHEESE BAKE

Servings: 3

1 (10.75 ounce) can cream of chicken soup

4 ounces plain yogurt

3/4 cups milk, divided

1 pound cooked chicken, cut into 1-inch chunks

1/4 teaspoon salt

1/2 teaspoon freshly ground black pepper

1/3 cup Bisquick

1/8 cup cornmeal

1 egg

1/2 cup cheddar cheese, shredded

1. In a 8 x 8 casserole dish, stir together soup, yogurt, and 1/2 cup milk. Mix well.
2. Add chicken, salt, and pepper and mix well.
3. In a bowl, mix together Bisquick, cornmeal, egg, and remaining milk. Pour over chicken mixture and mix gently to combine. Sprinkle with cheese.
4. Place pan on 1-inch rack. Baked, uncovered, on Power Level Hi (350 degrees F) for 15-17 minutes or until cheese is golden brown.

SPICY CHILI CHICKEN BREASTS

Try this if you like your food with a kick.

Servings: 4

4 chicken breasts
1/2 cup soy sauce, low-sodium
1 tablesoons olive oil
1 1/2 teaspoons curry powder
1 teaspoon garlic powder
1/2 teaspoon onion powder
1 teaspoon cayenne pepper

1. Place soy sauce, olive oil, curry powder, garlic powder, onion powder, and cayenne pepper in large resealable bag. Add chicken breasts, seal bag, and shake to coat chicken with marinade. Place in refrigerator to marinate for 2 hours or up to overnight.

2. Remove chicken from marinade and place on 3-inch rack. Cook on High power (350 degrees F) for 10 minutes.

3. Turn chicken over and brush with marinade. Cook for an additional 10 minutes or until chicken is cooked through and juices run clear. Discard remaining marinade.

TANDOORI CHICKEN SKEWERS

This chicken dish is packed with flavor. You can adjust the amount of spiciness you want by adding or reducing the amount of red pepper flakes.

Servings: 2

- **1/3 cup nonfat yogurt, plain**
- **1/4 cup lemon juice**
- **2 garlic cloves, crushed**
- **1 tablespoon paprika**
- **1/2 teaspoon curry powder**
- **1/2 teaspoon ground ginger**
- **1/2 teaspoon red pepper flakes**
- **2 chicken breasts, skinless and boneless, cut into 2-inch chunks**
- **4 6-inch skewers (soaked in water if using wooden skewers)**

1. In a bowl, combine yogurt, lemon juice, garlic, and spices. Blend well.
2. Divide chicken evenly and thread onto skewers. Place skewers in shallow baking or casserole dish. Pour yogurt mixture onto chicken. Cover and refrigerate for 1-2 hours or overnight.
3. Place chicken skewers on 3-inch rack. Bake at 350 degrees (High power) for 12 minutes, rotate skewers and bake for an additional 12 minutes or until chicken is cooked through and juices run clear.

CHICKEN ENCHILADA BAKE

This is a cheesy dish that is sure to be a crowd pleaser.
Servings: 4

2 cups cooked chicken, cut into bites-size pieces
1 can cream of chicken soup
1 1/2 cups shredded Mexican cheese, divided
1/2 (10 ounce) can chopped tomatoes and green chilies
1/2 can green chilies
1/8 cup fresh cilantro, chopped
3 large flour tortillas
1/2 cup corn, fresh or frozen
1/2 (15 ounce) can black beans, rinsed and drained
Optional toppings: chopped tomatoes, salsa, sour cream, avocado slices

1. Mix together chicken, soup, 1/2 cup shredded cheese, tomatoes, and cilantro.
2. Spray 8 x8 casserole dish with cooking spray.
3. Add 1/2 cup of filling to bottom of casserole, spread evenly.
4. Next, layer ingredients on top: tortilla, 1 cup filling, corn, beans, tortilla, 1 cup filling, corn, beans, tortilla. Top with shredded cheese.
5. Cover with aluminum foil, place on 1-inch rack and cook on High (350 degrees F) for 10 minutes. Uncover and cook for an addition 5-7 minutes or until cheese is golden brown and casserole is heated through.

CHICKEN, BROCCOLI, AND RICE BAKE

Servings: 4

3 chicken breasts, boneless and skinless, cut into 1-2 inch pieces
1 bag broccoli florets (fresh or frozen)
1 cup rice, uncooked
1 can cream of mushroom soup
2 cups chicken broth
1 teaspoon garlic powder
Salt and freshly ground black pepper, to taste
½ cup crushed Ritz cracker crumbs

1. Place all ingredients except for cracker crumbs into 8 x8 baking dish. Stir to combine. Sprinkle with cracker crumbs.
2. Place pan on 1-inch rack.
3. Bake on Power Level High (375 degrees F in Elite) for 20-22 minutes or until chicken is cooked through.

TERIYAKI WINGS

These moist, flavorful, wings can be on your table in about 30 minutes.
Servings: 4

½ cup soy sauce
½ cup honey
¼ cup orange juice
2 tablespoons rice vinegar
1 teaspoon arrowroot flour
1 tablespoon fresh ginger, grated
2 cloves garlic, minced
1 tablespoon sesame oil
1 teaspoon red pepper flakes
Oil, for greasing pan
1 ½ pounds chicken wings
Chopped green onions for garnish

1. Combine all ingredients through red pepper flakes in a bowl. Add chicken wings and mix well. Marinate in refrigerator for 2 hours or overnight.
2. Remove chicken wings from marinade and place on 1-inch rack. Reserve marinade.
3. Cook on High power (350 degrees F) for 15 minutes.
4. Pour reserved marinade in baking pan. Place chicken wings in baking dish in single layer. Stir to coat chicken with marinade.
5. Bake in oven for an additional 15 minutes or until chicken is cooked through (internal temperature should reach 165 degrees).
6. Remove from oven immediately. Garnish with green onions.

CRUNCHY-SPICY BAKED CHICKEN DRUMSTICKS

These crunchy chicken legs are so easy to prepare yet so tasty they're sure to become a family favorite.

Servings: 4

- 12 chicken drumsticks
- 2 tablespoons olive oil or coconut oil
- 1/2 flour
- 1 teaspoon garlic powder
- 1 teaspoon paprika
- 1 teaspoon cayenne pepper
- Salt and freshly ground black pepper, to taste

1. Using basting brush, coat chicken with olive oil or coconut oil.
2. In a large bowl, combine flour, garlic powder, paprika, cayenne pepper, salt, and pepper.
3. Add chicken to bowl and toss until chicken is covered with seasonings.
4. Arrange drumsticks on 4-inch rack. Cook on High power (350 degrees F) for 12 minutes. Turn drumsticks over and cook for an additional 12-15 minutes.

JUST LIKE KFC NUWAVE OVEN-FRIED CHICKEN

Crispy and crunchy!
Serves: 3-4

½ cup flour

½ cup cornstarch

½ cup Panko breadcrumbs

½ teaspoon salt

1 tablespoon seasoning salt (like Lawry's)

½ tsp pepper

2 tsp paprika

3 chicken breasts, cut in strips

4-5 tablespoooon butter, melted

1. Combine flour, cornstarch, breadcrumbs, salt, seasoning salt, pepper, and paprika in large resealable plastic bag.

2. Brush each piece of chicken with melted butter and then place in plastic bag. Shake gently to coat chicken thoroughly. This can be done in several batches. Remove chicken pieces from bag and place on baking sheet.

3. Place on 1-inch rack and cook on High power (350 degrees F) for 7 minutes. Turn chicken pieces over and brush with a little more melted butter. Cook for another 7-8 minutes until chicken is crispy and cooked through. Remove from oven and place on wire rack until ready to serve.

HOT AND SPICY BAKED BUFFALO CHICKEN WINGS

Servings: 4

½ cup butter melted
½ cup Frank's Red Hot Sauce (or other red pepper sauce)
1 tablespoon white vinegar
½ teaspoon Worcestershire sauce
¾ cup flour
¾ cup cornmeal
¼ teaspoon cayenne pepper
¼ teaspoon garlic powder
Salt and pepper, to taste
1 ½ pounds chicken wings, cut at joint

1. Combine melted butter, Frank's Hot Sauce, vinegar, and Worcestershire sauce in saucepan over low heat. Whisk together until well blended simmer on low while chicken wings cook.
2. In large bowl, combine flour, cornmeal, cayenne pepper, garlic powder, salt, and pepper. Add wings and turn to coat evenly.
3. Place wings on 4-inch rack. Cook on High power (350 degrees F) for 8 minutes. Turn over and cook for an additional 8-10 minutes, until wings are cooked through and juices run clear.
4. Remove wings promptly from Nuwave Oven and dip, in batches, into buffalo sauce until thoroughly coated. Place on serving dish and serve with celery sticks and blue cheese dressing.

GARLIC GINGER CHICKEN WINGS

Another take on spicy wings, this time with the zing of ginger.
Servings: 4

1 tablespoon Frank's Red Hot Sauce (or other red pepper sauce)
1 tablespoon vegetable oil
Salt and black pepper, to taste
1 ½ pounds chicken wings, cut at joint
1/3 cup flour
For glaze:
3 garlic cloves, crushed
1 tablespoon fresh ginger, minced
1 tablespoon Asian chili pepper sauce
¼ cup rice wine vinegar
¼ cup brown sugar, packed
1 tablespoon soy sauce

1. In a large mixing bowl, combine Frank's Red Hot Sauce, vegetable oil, salt and pepper. Add chicken wings and toss to coat thoroughly.
2. Place coated wings in large zip lock bag. Add flour, seal bag and shake until wings are coated with flour.
3. Place wings on 4-inch rack and cook on High power (350 degrees F) for 10 minutes. Turn wings over and cook for an additional 8 minutes.
4. In large bowl, whisk together all ingredients for glaze. Place wings in glaze and toss to coat evenly. Place wings back on 4-inch rack and cook on High power for an additional 5 minutes.
5. Remove from oven and serve.

OVEN FRIED CHICKEN WINGS

Servings: 4

Cooking spray
1/3 cup Parmesan cheese
1/3 cup panko-style bread crumbs
1/8 teaspoon garlic powder
1/8 teaspoon onion powder
1/8 teaspoon ground black pepper
Pinch of salt
1/4 cup melted butter
1 ½ pounds chicken wings, split at joint

1. Spray baking sheet with cooking spray.
2. In bowl, mix together Parmesan cheese, bread crumbs, garlic powder, onion powder, black pepper, and salt.
3. One at a time, dip chicken wings into melted butter and then into bread mixture until thoroughly coated. Arrange wings in single layer on baking sheet.
4. Place on 1-inch rack and cook on High power (350 degrees F) for 10 minutes. Turn wings over and cook for an additional 10-12 minutes until no longer pink in center and juices run clear. Remove promptly from NuWave Oven.

JERK CHICKEN WINGS

Hot, flavorful, and addictively delicious.
Servings: 4

¼ cup orange juice
1 ½ tablespoons lemon juice
1 ½ tablespoons lime juice
1 tablespoon fresh thyme, chopped or ½ tablespoon dried thyme
2 cloves garlic, minced
1 tablespoon fresh ginger, minced or ½ tablespoon dried ginger
1 small jalapeno or habanero pepper, seeded and chopped
1 tablespoon cumin
½ teaspoon allspice
¼ teaspoon nutmeg
¼ teaspoon cinnamon
½ teaspoon salt
2 teaspoons freshly ground black pepper
1/3 cup olive oil
1 ½ pounds chicken wings, cut at joint

1. In a bowl, mix together all ingredients through black pepper. Whisk in the olive oil. Pour ¾ of the marinade into large resealable zip lock bag. Reserve remaining marinade. Add chicken wings to bag, seal, and shake bag to coat chicken wings. Place in refrigerator for 4 hours or overnight. Refrigerate remaining marinade.
2. Remove chicken wings from marinade and place on 4-inch rack. Cook on High power (350 degrees F) for 10 minutes. Turn wings over, baste with reserved marinade and cook for an additional 10-12 minutes or until no longer pink in center and juices run clear. Remove promptly from NuWave Oven.

BACON AND CHICKEN KABOBS

Servings: 4

1/3 cup soy sauce
1/3 cup cider vinegar
1 tablespoon honey
1 ½ tablespoons olive oil
1 green onion, minced
8 large mushrooms, halved
2 skinless, boneless chicken breasts, cut into chunks
½ pound bacon slices, cut in half
1 cup fresh pineapple chunks
Wooden skewers, soaked for 20-30 minutes in water

1. Line bottom of Nuwave Oven with foil for easy clean-up.
2. Mix together soy sauce, cider vinegar, honey, olive oil, and green onions in a bowl. Pour into large resealable plastic bag. Add mushrooms and chicken to marinade, seal, and shake bag to coat. Place in refrigerator for at least 2 hours.
3. Remove chicken and mushrooms from marinade. Pour remaining marinade in small saucepan and bring to boil. Reduce heat and simmer while kabobs cook.
4. Wrap each piece of chicken with a slice of bacon and thread onto skewers along with mushrooms and pineapple.
5. Arrange skewers on 4-inch rack. Cook on High power (350 degrees F) for 8 minutes. Turn kabobs over and cook for an additional 8-10 minutes.
6. Remove kabobs from NuWave Oven and serve topped with additional marinade.

GRILLED CHICKEN SALAD WITH MANGO AND AVOCADO

This makes a nice light supper on a summer night.
Servings: 4

2 tablespoons olive oil, divided
Juice of 1 lime
1 tablespoon honey
1 teaspoon fresh ginger, grated
4 skinless, boneless chicken breasts
2 mangoes, peeled and diced
2 avocados, peeled and diced
8 cups mixed salad greens
1 tablespoon balsamic vinegar

1. In a small bowl, combine 1 tablespoon olive oil, lime, honey, and ginger.
2. Place chicken on plate and brush each side with oil mixture.
3. Place chicken breasts on 4-inch rack and cook on High power (350 degrees F) for 10 minutes. When timer beeps, flip chicken over and cook for an additional 10-12 minutes until chicken is no longer pink inside and juices run clear. Leave lid on and let chicken rest for an additional 10 minutes.
4. Remove chicken from oven and slice into strips.
5. Add salad greens to large salad bowl. Add sliced chicken, mango, and avocado. Drizzle with remaining olive oil and balsamic vinegar.

JUICY WHOLE ROASTED CHICKEN

Cooked to perfection in the NuWave Oven.
Servings: 6

1 whole chicken (3-4 pounds)
1 onion, chopped
½ lemon
3-4 garlic cloves
2 tablespoons olive oil
1 teaspoon paprika
1 teaspoon dried thyme
½ teaspoon salt
½ teaspoon freshly ground black pepper

1. Wash chicken and pat dry. Place whole chicken on 1-inch rack. Insert chopped onion, lemon, and garlic cloves. Brush chicken with olive oil and sprinkle with remaining seasonings.
2. Roast on High power (350 degrees F) for 15-17 minutes per pound, turning chicken over halfway through cooking. Chicken is done when internal temperature reaches 180 degrees F. Allow chicken to rest for 10 minutes before slicing for serving.

Note: Chicken can also be cooked directly from frozen. If frozen, allow for 26-28 minutes per pound.

BACON-WRAPPED CHICKEN WITH POTATOES

Servings: 4

4 chicken drumsticks
4 chicken thighs
8 slices bacon
1 pound baby red potatoes
1 tablespoons dried basil
1/2 tablespoon garlic powder
1/2 tablespoon adobo seasoning
1/2 tablespoon freshly ground black pepper
1 teaspoon salt

1. Wrap each piece of chicken with one slice of bacon.
2. Line bottom of NuWave Oven with foil.
3. Arrange chicken in center of 4-inch rack. Place potatoes around chicken on rack.
4. In a small bowl, mix together basil, garlic powder, adobo seasoning, black pepper, and salt. Sprinkle seasoning mixture over chicken and potatoes.
5. Cook on High Power (350 degrees F) for 10 minutes. Turn chicken and potatoes over and cook for an additional 10 minutes or until chicken is cooked through and potatoes are tender.

NUWAVE THAI COCONUT CHICKEN

This chicken turns out flavorful and juicy.
Servings: 4

2-inch piece of fresh ginger, peeled and sliced thin
1 scallion, chopped
Juice of 1 lemon
3 garlic cloves
1 cup fresh cilantro, packed
¾ cup coconut milk, unsweetened
¾ cup pork marinade (Stubb's or similar)
1 tablespoon soy sauce
¼ cup dark brown sugar, packed
½ teaspoon salt
2 1/2 pounds boneless, skinless chicken thighs or breasts

1. Place all ingredients except for chicken into food processor or blender. Pulse several times to combine. Pour marinade into large resealable bag.
2. Place chicken in bag, seal, and shake gently. Place in refrigerator for 2 hours or overnight.
3. Remove chicken from marinade and place on 4-inch rack.
4. Cook on High power (350 degrees F) for 7 minutes. Turn chicken over and cook for an additional 7-8 minutes or until juices run clear.

PESTO CHICKEN WITH PROSCIUTTO AND GOUDA

Delicious and elegant dish that is simple to prepare.
Servings: 4

4 boneless, skinless chicken breasts
1 teaspoon garlic powder
Salt and freshly ground black pepper, to taste
½ cup basil pesto
4 thin slices prosciutto
8 thin slices smoked gouda cheese

1. Pound each chicken breast with wooden mallet until even. Sprinkle with garlic powder, salt, and pepper. Spread about 1 tablespoon of pesto on each chicken breast. Top with slice of prosciutto and 2 slices of gouda cheese. Roll up chicken breast and secure with toothpick.
2. Place chicken breasts on 10-inch baking dish and place on 1-inch rack.
3. Bake on High Power (350 degrees F) for 10 minutes. Turn chicken breasts over and cook for an additional 8-10 minutes or until chicken is cooked through.

APPLE-STUFFED CHICKEN BREAST

Servings: 4

2 skinless, boneless chicken breasts
1 large apple, chopped (Granny Smith, Rome, Gala, or Golden Delicious)
2 tablespoons cheddar cheese, shredded
1 tablespoon panko-style bread crumbs
2 tablespoons pecans, chopped
2 tablespoons brown sugar
1 teaspoon ground cinnamon
½ teaspoon curry powder

1. In bowl, combine apple, cheese, breadcrumbs, pecans, brown sugar, cinnamon, and curry powder.

2. Pound chicken breasts between sheets of waxed paper until about 1/4-inch thick.

3. Spread half of apple mixture on each chicken breast. Roll up chicken and secure with toothpicks.

4. Place chicken on 4-inch rack and cook on High power for 12 minutes. Turn over and cook for an additional 10-12 minutes.

SOUTHWEST-STYLE TURKEY BURGERS

Turkey burgers with a spicy kick.

Servings: 4

1 ½ pounds ground turkey

2 cloves garlic, minced

¼ red onion, finely chopped

½ red bell pepper, finely chopped

1 jalapeno pepper, seeded and diced

2 tablespoons fresh cilantro, chopped

2 teaspoons ground cumin

1 teaspoon hot sauce

2 teaspoons steak seasoning

4 slices pepper jack cheese

8 slices crusty French bread, or bun, toasted lightly

Salsa, for topping

Lettuce, for topping

1. In bowl, combine ground turkey, garlic, red onion, bell pepper, jalapeno pepper, cilantro, cumin, hot sauce, and steak seasoning. Form mixture into 4 patties, about ¾-inch thick.
2. Place burgers on 3-inch rack and cook on High power (350 degrees F) for 6 minutes. Flip burgers over and cook for an additional 5 minutes. Top each burger with slice of pepper jack cheese and cook for an additional 1-2 minutes to melt cheese.
3. Place each burger on slice of French bread, top with salsa and lettuce, and additional slice of bread.

HERB-ROASTED TURKEY BREAST

Juicy and flavorful, this is sure to be a hit with your family and friends.
Servings: 6

1 turkey breast, about 6-7 pounds
3-4 cloves garlic, minced
2 teaspoons dry mustard
1/2 tablespoon dried rosemary
1/2 tablespoon dried sage
1/2 tablespoon dried thyme
2 teaspoons sea salt
1 teaspoon freshly ground black pepper
2 tablespoons olive oil
2 tablespoons lemon juice

1. In small bowl, combine garlic, dry mustard, rosemary, sage, thyme, salt, pepper, olive oil, and lemon juice. Brush mixture on turkey breast, spreading evenly.
2. Place turkey breast on 1-inch rack. Roast on High power (350 degrees F) for 35-40 minutes. Turn turkey breast over and roast for an additional 35-40 minutes. If turkey is getting too crisp, place foil over top. Use meat thermometer to ensure meat reaches 180 degrees F. Allow turkey to sit for 10 minutes before slicing.

5
PORK

Pork is very versatile and always come out perfectly in the NuWave Oven.

CUBAN-STYLE PORK LOIN

This works great for making Cuban sandwiches.
Servings: 4

4 cloves garlic, minced
1 teaspoon salt
1 teaspoon ground black pepper
1 teaspoon ground cumin
1 teaspoon oregano
1 teaspoon coriander
½ cup orange juice
¼ cup lime juice
2 tablespoons olive oil
1 teaspoon white wine vinegar
1 ½ pound pork loin roast

1. In a bowl, whisk together all ingredients through white wine vinegar. Pour into large zip lock bag and add pork loin. Place in refrigerator and marinate for a minimum of 4 hours or overnight.
2. Remove roast from zip lock bag and reserve marinade.
3. Place pork on 4-inch rack. Cook on power level High (350 degrees F) for 15 minutes. Turn roast over and cook for an additional 15 minutes or until internal temperature is 160 to 170 degrees F.
4. While pork is cooking, simmer marinade in small pan over medium heat, stirring occasionally. Remove roast from NuWave Oven, place on platter, and drizzle with marinade.

ITALIAN SAUSAGE CASSEROLE

Easy and economical one-dish meal.
Servings: 4

1 pound Italian sausages, casings removed

4 medium potatoes, peeled and cubed

2 large carrots, sliced

1 medium yellow onions, chopped

2 (15 ounce cans) seasoned chopped tomatoes

1 teaspoon sea salt

1 teaspoon freshly ground black pepper

1/2 teaspoon dried oregano

1/2 teaspoon garlic powder

1. Cut sausage into 1-inch pieces. Sauté in medium skillet over medium-high heat until browned. Remove from skillet and place in 8 x 8 casserole dish.
2. Add potatoes, carrots, and onions over sausage. Pour chopped tomatoes on top. Season with salt, pepper, and oregano.
3. Place pan on 1-inch rack and cook on High (350 degrees F) for 35-40 minutes.

HONEY-GINGER PORK CHOPS

These pork chops are very flavorful.
Servings: 4

4 boneless pork chops
¼ cup cider vinegar
3 cup honey
2 cloves garlic, minced
½ teaspoon ground ginger
1 1/2 tablespoons soy sauce
½ teaspoon freshly ground black pepper

1. In a bowl, combine all ingredients except pork chops.
2. Pour into large zipper lock bag and add pork chops. Seal and shake to coat pork chops. Place in refrigerator for a minimum of 1 hour.
3. Place pork chops on 4-inch rack. Cook on High (350 degrees F) for 5 minutes per side or until pork reaches internal temperature of 160 degrees.

EASY PEASY HAM AND CHEESE CASSEROLE

This recipe is bound to be a hit with even your pickiest eaters.

Servings: 4

- **1 1/2 cups milk**
- **1 (10.75 ounce) can cream of mushroom soup**
- **2 cups cooked ham, diced**
- **2 cups bowtie pasta, cooked**
- **1 cup green peas, fresh or frozen**
- **1/2 medium yellow onion, chopped**
- **1/2 cup shredded cheese, cheddar or Monterey Jack**
- **1/2 cup bread crumbs (panko-style is preferred)**

1. Pour milk and soup into 8 x8 casserole dish. Stir together to combine. Add in ham, pasta, peas, and onion. Stir to combine. Sprinkle with cheese and bread crumbs.
2. Place on 1-inch rack and bake, covered with foil, on Power Level High (350 degrees F) for 25 minutes. Uncover, and bake an additional 10 minutes or until cheese is golden brown.

APPLE BUTTER PORK TENDERLOIN

This needs to marinate overnight, but is definitely worth the wait.
Servings: 4

1 (1 lb) pork tenderloin
1/4 teaspoon dried thyme
1/8 teaspoon mustard powder
2 cloves garlic, minced
4 tablespoons soy sauce
4 tablespoons sherry wine
For the Sauce
6 tablespoons apple butter
1 tablespoon sherry wine
1 tablespoon soy sauce
3/4 teaspoon garlic salt, to taste

1. Combine thyme, garlic, mustard powder, sherry, and soy sauce in a gallon-size zipper lock bag. Add the tenderloin and marinate in the refrigerator for minimum of 4 hours, preferably overnight.
2. Remove tenderloin from bag, discard marinade, and place in roasting pan.
3. Combine the apple butter, sherry, soy sauce, and garlic salt in bowl.
4. Cover pork with the apple butter mixture.
5. Place tenderloin on 4-inch rack and cook on High (350 degrees F) for 10 to 12 minutes per side.

GLAZED PORK CHOPS WITH APRICOT-MANGO SALSA

These pork chops are so easy to prepare and mouth-wateringly good.

Servings: 4

1/3 cup Dijon mustard

3 tablespoons balsamic vinegar

1 teaspoon cumin

Salt and fresh ground black pepper, to taste

4 pork chops

For the Apricot-Mango Salsa

4 fresh apricots, pit removed, diced

1 ripe mango, peeled, diced

1/4 red onion, diced small

1/4 cup fresh basil, minced

1/4 cup extra virgin olive oil

1 teaspoon cardamom

1. In a bowl, mix mustard, vinegar, and cumin.
2. Sprinkle both sides of pork chops with salt and pepper. Brush mustard mixture onto pork chops, covering both sides.
3. Place pork chops on 4-inch rack and cook on High power (350 degrees F) for 5 minutes per side. Baste with mustard sauce when they're flipped.
4. While pork chops are cooking, mix together ingredients for relish in a bowl.
5. When pork chops are finished, top with salsa.

BACON-WRAPPED PORK MEDALLIONS

Servings: 4

8 slices bacon
1 ½ pound pork tenderloin, trimmed and cut into 8 medallions
1 tablespoon garlic powder
1/2 teaspoon salt
1 teaspoon dried oregano
1 tablespoon butter, melted
1 tablespoon olive oil

1. Line bottom of Nuwave Oven with foil.
2. Wrap each medallion with 1 slice of bacon, securing with a toothpick.
3. In small shallow bowl, combine garlic powder, salt, and oregano.
4. Dip each medallion in seasoning mix, turning to coat both sides.
5. Mix together melted butter and olive oil. Brush each side of medallions with butter and oil mixture.
6. Place medallions on 4-inch rack and cook on Power Level High (350 degrees F) for 8 minutes. Flip medallions over and cook for an additional 6 minutes or until bacon is crispy and pork reaches an internal temperature of 145 degrees F.

CANDIED BACON JERKY

Sweet and a little spicy.
Servings: 4

¾ cup brown sugar

½ teaspoon cayenne pepper

1 pound bacon

1. Combine brown sugar and cayenne pepper in shallow dish. Dip each slice of bacon into mixture, covering both sides.
2. Place bacon on 3-inch rack. Cook on Power Level 4 (175 degrees F) for 2 ½-3 hours, flipping bacon once or twice during cooking.

TERIYAKI PORK KABOBS

Quick, easy, and delicious!
Servings: 6

½ cup teriyaki sauce (i.e., Kikkoman)
2 tablespoons olive oil
2 pounds pork tenderloin, cut into 1-inch cubes
1 cup fresh pineapple, cut into 1-inch cubes
1 pint cherry tomatoes
12 button mushrooms, stems removed
1 bell pepper, cut into 1 ½-inch pieces
1 red onion, cut into 1 ½-inch pieces
Wooden skewers, soaked for 20-30 minutes in water

1. Whisk together teriyaki sauce and olive oil. Place pork cubes in bowl and pour marinade over it. Place in refrigerator and let pork marinate for a minimum of 1 hour, turning occasionally.

2. Remove pork from marinade (reserve remaining marinade) and thread onto skewers, alternating with different vegetables and pineapple.

3. Line bottom of NuWave Oven with foil.

4. Place kabobs on 4-inch rack. Brush with remaining marinade. Cook on High Power (350 degrees F) for 12 minutes. Turn kabobs over and cook for an additional 8-10 minutes or until desired doneness is reached.

5. Remove from oven, plate, and serve.

BARBECUE RIBS

Delicious!
Servings: 4

2 pounds pork spareribs
1 teaspoon sea salt
½ teaspoon paprika
1/8 teaspoon cayenne pepper
1/4 teaspoon garlic powder
1/2 cup brown sugar
1/8 cup Worcestershire sauce
1/8 cup ketchup
1/8 cup soy sauce
1/4 cup chili sauce
2 cloves garlic, minced
1/2 teaspoon dry mustard
1/2 teaspoon ground black pepper

1. Cut ribs into serving size portions.
2. In a small bowl, mix together salt, paprika, cayenne pepper, and garlic powder. Rub this onto pork ribs.
3. Mix together brown sugar, Worcestershire sauce, ketchup, soy sauce, chili sauce, garlic, dry mustard, and ground pepper.
4. Brush marinade over ribs, coating thoroughly. Cover and marinate for a minimum of 1 hour over overnight in refrigerator.
5. Place ribs on 4-inch rack and cook on High power (350 degrees) for 6 minutes. Turn over and cook for an additional 5-6 minutes.

CHINESE-STYLE BARBECUED PORK

You will be surprised how easy it is to make this Chinese-style pork in the NuWave Oven.

Servings: 4

½ tablespoon brown sugar
2 tablespoons honey, divided
1 ½ tablespoons hoisin sauce
1 1/2 tablespoons soy sauce
½ teaspoon five spice powder
1 pound pork tenderloin

1. Whisk together brown sugar, 1 tablespoon honey, hoisin sauce, soy sauce, and five spice powder in a bowl. Pour into large resealable plastic bag. Add pork tenderloin to bag, seal, and shake to coat pork. Place in refrigerator to marinate for a minimum of 3 hours and preferably overnight.
2. Remove pork from marinade (reserve marinade). Add remaining 1 tablespoon honey to marinade and stir until well blended.
3. Place pork on 3-inch rack. Cook on Power Level High (350 degrees F) for 10 minutes. Baste pork with marinade, turn over, baste again, and cook for an additional 10-12 minutes.
4. Remove pork from NuWave Oven and allow to rest for 5 minutes before slicing.

PARMESAN-CRUSTED PORK CHOPS

If you are looking for a new way to cook pork chops, try these!

Servings: 5

1/3 cup Parmesan cheese

2 tablespoons panko style breadcrumbs

1 tablespoon Italian seasoning

¼ teaspoon paprika

½ teaspoon garlic powder

Salt and freshly ground black pepper, to taste

4 pork chops, medium thickness

1 tablespoon olive oil

1. Spray 3-inch rack with cooking spray.

2. In a shallow bowl or plate mix together Parmesan cheese, bread crumbs, Italian seasoning, paprika, garlic powder, salt, and pepper.

3. Lightly brush each side of pork chops with olive oil and then dip in seasoning mixture.

4. Place pork chops on 3-inch rack. Bake on High power (350 degrees F) for 6 minutes, flip over and cook for an additional 6-8 minutes or until pork chops reach an internal temperature of 160 degrees F.

6
Beef and Lamb

YUMMY HOMESTYLE MEATLOAF

Comfort food at its best.
Servings: 4

1 tablespoon olive oil
1 large yellow onion, diced
3 garlic cloves, minced
¾ pound ground beef
¾ pound ground pork
2 tablespoons tomato paste
1/2 cup bread crumbs
2 large eggs
1 tablespoon oregano
Salt and freshly ground black pepper, to taste
1 can (8 ounce) tomato sauce

1. In a medium pan, heat olive oil over medium-high heat. Add onion and garlic and sauté for 3-4 minutes. remove from heat and set aside.
2. In a large bowl, combine ground beef, ground pork, onion mixture, tomato paste, almond flour, eggs, oregano, salt, and pepper. Mix together with fork.
3. Brush shallow baking dish with olive oil. Place ground meat mixture in center of pan and form into loaf shape.
4. Place pan on 1-inch rack and cook on High power (350 degrees F) for 40 minutes. Cover with foil and cook for an additional 5 minutes. Remove foil, spread tomato sauce on top of loaf. Cook for an additional 5 minutes.

FRENCH ONION MEATLOAF

Servings: 6

- 2 pounds lean ground beef
- 1/2 cup rolled oats
- 1/2 cup panko bread crumbs
- ½ onion, finely chopped
- 2 eggs, lightly beaten
- 1 can (10.5 oz) French onion soup
- 1 teaspoon dried thyme
- 1/2 teaspoon ground black pepper
- 1 cup shredded Swiss or gruyere cheese
- ¼ cup grated Parmesan cheese
- 1 can crispy fried onions

1. In a large bowl, combine beef, oats, bread crumbs, onion, eggs, French onion soup, thyme, and black pepper until well mixed.
2. Form into loaf and place into loaf pan coated with cooking spray.
3. Place on 1-inch rack and cook on High power (350 degrees F) for 40 minutes. Remove meatloaf from oven and top with shredded cheese, Parmesan cheese, and fried onions. Cook for an additional 10-15 minutes until cheese is melted. Allow to cool for 5-10 minutes before serving.

BEEF AND VEGGIE KABOBS WITH SPICY MEDITERRANEAN MARINADE

The spicy marinade gives the meat and veggies a nice kick.
Servings: 4

Marinade
1/3 cup olive oil
2 tablespoons tomato paste
5 cloves garlic, minced
1 tablespoon lemon juice
1 tablespoon honey
1 teaspoon salt
1/2 teaspoon cumin
1/2 teaspoon paprika
1/2 teaspoon coriander
1/2 teaspoon freshly ground pepper

Kebabs
1 pound sirloin, cut into 1-inch cubes
1/2 pound mushrooms, stems trimmed
1 medium summer squash, cut into 1-inch chunks
1 medium red onion, cut into 1-inch chunks
1 bell pepper, cut into 1-inch chunks
1 carton grape tomatoes
8 (8-inch) skewers (if using wooden skewers, soak in water for 30 minutes before using)

1. In a large bowl, whisk together all of the ingredients for the marinade. Put 1/4 cup of the marinade into a large zip lock bag. Add the beef cubes to the bag, seal it, and shake bag to thoroughly coat beef with marinade. Set aside and allow beef to marinate for at least thirty minutes up to overnight.
2. Add the vegetables to the bowl with marinade. Stir to coat the vegetables with marinade. Thread the vegetables onto 4 skewers, alternating between type of vegetables. Allow a little space between each piece. Reserve remaining marinade for basting.
3. When beef is ready, thread onto 4 skewers, leaving a little space between each piece.
4. Place skewers on 4-inch rack. Cook on High power (350 degrees F for 5 minutes. Baste with marinade, turn over and cook for an additional 4 to 6 minutes or to desired doneness.
5. Serve immediately.

GRILLED STEAK WITH GINGER MARINADE

This recipe is very simple, but oh so delicious.
Servings: 4

1 piece of fresh ginger (about 6-inches), sliced into thin slices
1/4 cup sesame oil
8 cloves garlic, minced
2 teaspoons lemon juice
1 tablespoon honey
2 teaspoons salt
1 teaspoon freshly ground pepper
1 1/2 pounds flank steak, trimmed

1. In a bowl, whisk together all ingredients except steak. Pour into large resealable plastic bag. Add flank steak, seal, and shake to thoroughly coat steak with marinade.
2. Allow to marinade for 30 minutes at room temperature. Can also marinate in refrigerator for up to 24 hours.
3. Remove steak from marinade, allow excess marinade to drip off. Ensure liner is at base of oven and place steak on 4-inch rack. Cook steaks on High power until desired doneness, flipping once during cooking. For rare, cook 5-6 minutes per side; for medium rare, cook 6-7 minutes per side; for medium, cook 7-8 minutes per side, and for well done cook 9-10 minutes per side. Insert meat thermometer to check for doneness.
4. Remove from oven and place on cutting board and let rest for 5-10 minutes. Slice, against the grain, into thin slices. Serve.

BEEF ROAST

Simple and cooked to perfection.
Servings: 4-6

3 pounds beef eye of round roast
½ teaspoon sea salt
½ teaspoon garlic powder
¼ teaspoon freshly ground black pepper

1. Allow roast to come to room temperature before cooking.
2. Tie roast at three-inch intervals with twine. Place roast in pan and season with salt, garlic powder, and black pepper.
3. Place on 1-inch rack and roast on High power (350 degrees F) for 15 minutes per pound for rare, 20 minutes per pound for medium, and 23 minutes per pound for well-done. Confirm doneness with meat thermometer.
4. Remove from oven, cover loosely with foil and allow roast to rest for 15 minutes before slicing.

GRUYERE MUSHROOM BURGERS

Tasty and juicy burgers topped with cheese and mushrooms.
Servings: 4

1 ½ pounds ground beef
Sea salt and freshly ground black pepper, to taste
½ teaspoon garlic powder
1 small red onion, cut in half and sliced thin
8 ounces mushrooms, sliced
1 tablespoon olive oil
1 tablespoon Worcestershire sauce
¼ cup ketchup
2 teaspoons Dijon mustard
4 slices gruyere cheese
4 sesame buns
Lettuce and tomato for topping, if desired

1. Place ground beef in bowl and season with salt, pepper, and garlic powder. Mix gently. Form into 4 patties, about 3/4-inch thick. Place burgers in refrigerator to chill while preparing onions and mushrooms.
2. Add sliced onions and mushrooms in liner pan. Drizzle with olive oil and Worcestershire sauce. Stir to coat vegetables. Cook mixture on High power (350 degrees F) for 10 minutes. Remove from oven and cover with foil to keep warm while burgers cook.
3. In small bowl, mix together ketchup and mustard and set aside.
4. Place burgers on 3-inch rack and cook for 5-7 minutes. Flip burgers over and cook for an additional 4-6 minutes. Top each burger with one-quarter of onion and mushroom mixture and slice of gruyere cheese and cook for an additional 1-2 minutes until cheese is melted.
5. Spread ketchup mixture onto buns, top with burgers, lettuce, and tomato.

EASY, TASTY LAMB CHOPS

These lamb chops can be made start to finish in less than half hour.

Servings: 4

2 garlic cloves, crushed

1 tablespoon rosemary, crushed

1 teaspoon thyme

2 tablespoons Dijon mustard

2 tablespoons lemon juice plus additional slices for garnish

3 tablespoons olive oil

4 lamb chops (about 1-inch thick)

Salt and freshly ground black pepper, to taste

1. In a bowl, combine garlic, rosemary, thyme, mustard, lemon juice, and 1 tablespoon of the olive oil. Stir until well blended. Spread mixture over lamb chops, coating both sides thoroughly. Let marinate for 20 minutes at room temperature.

2. Place lamb chops on 3- or 4-inch rack. Cook on High power (350 degrees F) for 3 minutes. Flip chops over and cook for an additional 3-4 minutes or until desired level of doneness. Serve garnished with lemon slices.

GREEK-STYLE LAMB KABOBS

These lamb kabobs are a flavorful blend of herbs, spices, and garlic.
Servings: 4

½ cup olive oil
1/3 cup lemon juice
4 garlic cloves, minced
1 teaspoon ground coriander
1 teaspoon ground cumin
1 teaspoon salt
2 teaspoons ground black pepper
1 ½ pounds boneless leg of lamb, cut into 1-inch cubes
1 red onion, cut into 1 ½-inch chunks
Wooden skewers, soaked for 20-30 in water

1. In a bowl, whisk together olive oil, lemon juice, garlic, coriander, cumin, salt, and pepper. Add lamb cubes to bowl and toss to coat. Marinate for 2 hours or overnight in refrigerator.
2. Remove lamb from marinade and thread onto skewers along with onion.
3. Place skewers on 4-inch rack and cook on High Power (350 degrees F) for 6 minutes, turn and cook and addition 4-6 minutes or until desired degree of doneness is reached.
4. Serve with couscous or rice pilaf.

SPICY BEEF JERKY

Homemade beef jerky makes a delicious low-carb snack.

Servings: 4-5

1 pound beef round steak, cut into thin strips

1/8 cup soy sauce

1 tablespoon Worcestershire sauce

1 tablespoon liquid smoke

1 tablespoon brown sugar

1 teaspoon salt

1 teaspoon ground black pepper

½ teaspoon garlic powder

½ teaspoon onion powder

½ teaspoon cayenne pepper

½ teaspoon paprika

1. Place all ingredients in large recloseable plastic bag or container with lid. Mix to evenly coat beef strips. Place in refrigerator and marinate overnight (at least 8 hours).
2. Remove beef strips and arrange in liner pan and 3-inch rack.
3. Cook on Power level 4 (175 degrees F) for 3 to 3 ½ hours.

7
Seafood

Heart healthy seafood is easy and delicious in the NuWave Oven.

PANKO-CRUSTED COD

Panko are Japanese-style breadcrumbs and provide a crunchy taste. Available in most supermarkets.

Servings: 2

1/4 Panko-style breadcrumbs

1 clove garlic, minced

1 tablespoon extra-virgin olive oil

3 tablespoons nonfat Greek yogurt

1 tablespoon mayonnaise

1 1/2 teaspoons lemon juice

1/2 teaspoon tarragon

Pinch of salt

10 ounces cod, cut into two portions

1. Coat baking pan with nonstick cooking spray.
2. In a small bowl, combine breadcrumbs, garlic, and olive oil.
3. In another bowl, combine yogurt, mayonnaise, lemon juice, tarragon, and salt.
4. Place fish in baking pan. Top each piece with one half yogurt mixture and then 1/3 breadcrumb mixture.
5. Place pan on 3-inch rack and cook at 350 degrees F (High) for 13-15 minutes or until fish is opaque in center and breadcrumbs are golden brown.

GRILLED SALMON AND ASPARAGUS WITH LEMON BUTTER

Salmon is rich in heart-healthy omega-3s. Buy wild salmon whenever possible.

Servings: 4

1 1/4 pounds salmon, cut into 4 portions

2 bunches asparagus, ends trimmed

½ tablespoon olive oil

1/2 teaspoon salt

1/4 teaspoon freshly ground pepper

1/4 teaspoon garlic powder

1 tablespoon olive oil

1 tablespoon butter

3 tablespoons lemon juice

1. Place salmon and asparagus on baking sheet. Lightly brush with olive oil. Sprinkle with salt, pepper, and garlic powder.
2. Place asparagus and salmon on 3-inch rack. Cook at 350 degrees F (High) for 5-6 minutes, turn over and cook for an additional 4-5 minutes until salmon is opaque and asparagus is tender.
3. In a microwave-safe bowl, place olive oil, butter, and lemon juice. Microwave to melt butter, about 20 seconds. Drizzle fish with butter-lemon mixture. Serve immediately.

ORANGE MARMALADE MARINATED SALMON

Very tasty and different salmon recipe.

Servings: 4

- 2/3 cup orange marmalade
- 1/3 cup rice vinegar
- 1/3 cup soy sauce
- 1 teaspoon minced garlic
- 1 teaspoon grated fresh ginger
- 1 teaspoon onion powder
- 1 teaspoon sesame oil
- 1 teaspoon olive oil
- 1 pinch chili pepper flakes
- black pepper, to taste
- 2 pounds fresh salmon fillets
- Fresh sliced scallion (for garnish)

1. Add all ingredients except for salmon to gallon-size zipper lock plastic bag. Seal and shake to combine. Add salmon, reseal, and refrigerate for 1 hour to marinate.
2. Remove salmon from marinade and place on 4-inch rack.
3. Cook on High (350 degrees F) for 5 minutes on each side or until center is opaque and fish flakes easily.

BAKED FISH WITH HERBED BACON

Servings: 2

1 pound fish (cod, halibut or bass), cut into 2 (8 oz.) pieces

1 tablespoon olive oil

1 teaspoon lemon juice

Pinch of cayenne pepper

salt and pepper, to taste

2 tablespoons butter

1 piece of bacon, browned, finely minced

2 teaspoon dried parsley

1 teaspoon dried basil

Pinch of garlic powder

Pinch of salt

1. Line a rimmed roasting sheet with parchment paper.
2. Place fish on prepared sheet. Brush with olive oil, drizzle with lemon juice and sprinkle cayenne pepper. Season it with salt and pepper to taste.
3. Place on 1-inch rack and cook on High power (350 degrees F) for 8-10 minutes, until fish flakes easily with fork.
4. Meanwhile, in a bowl combine bacon bits with butter, parsley, basil, garlic powder, salt and pepper; mix until well blended. Serve fish with bacon mixture on top.

FISH BAKED WITH TOMATOES AND POTATOES

This is an easy, one dish seafood dinner.
Servings: 4

1 1/2 lbs white fish fillets (cod, halibut or haddock)
4 small potatoes, peeled and thinly sliced
1/2 medium onion, thinly sliced
1/2 teaspoon salt
1/2 teaspoon pepper
1 (15 ounce) can diced tomatoes, seasoned with garlic and basil
2 tablespoons fresh parsley, chopped
1/2 teaspoon dried oregano

1. Place fish in 10 x 10 baking dish. Top with potatoes, onion, tomatoes, salt, pepper, parsley, and oregano.
2. Cover with foil and place on 1-inch rack.
3. Cook on High power (350 degrees F) for 12-15 minutes or until potatoes are tender and fish flakes easily.

SOY AND GINGER MAHI MAHI

Enjoy this Asian-inspired dish over rice.

Servings: 4

2 pounds mahi mahi fillets (4 medium pieces)
2 tablespoons olive oil
2 tablespoons fresh ginger, minced
1 tablespoon garlic, minced
1 tablespoon fresh lime juice
1/4 cup soy sauce
2 tablespoons honey
2 tablespoons dry red wine
1/8 teaspoon cayenne pepper
Salt and freshly ground black pepper, to taste

1. Combine all ingredients except for fish in a gallon-size zipper close plastic bag. Shake to combine.
2. Add fish, seal, and place in refrigerator to marinate for at least 4 hours or overnight.
3. Remove fish from marinade and place on 4-inch rack.
4. Cook on High power (350 degrees F) for 4 minutes, turn, and cook for another 2-3 minutes or until fish flakes easily.

CITRUS BAKED SALMON

Servings: 4

- 4 slices lemon
- 4 slices orange
- 4 salmon fillets (6-8 ounces each)
- Salt and freshly ground black pepper
- 2 tablespoons fresh dill, chopped
- 2 tablespoons sun-dried tomatoes
- 1 tablespoon olive oil
- 2/3 cup rice wine vinegar

1. Place lemon and orange slices, side by side, in the bottom of a shallow baking dish that will fit in NuWave oven (10 x10). Place each salmon fillet across the citrus slices. Sprinkle with salt and pepper.
2. In a small bowl, combine dill, sun-dried tomatoes, olive oil, and rice wine vinegar. Drizzle mixture over salmon fillets.
3. Place on 1-inch rack and cook on High power (350 degrees F) for 7-8 minutes or until salmon is cooked through.

WASABI SALMON BURGERS

Canned salmon are usually wild salmon that contain one of the highest amounts of omega-3s. Wasabi provides a distinct Japanese treat.

Servings: 4

- 1/2 teaspoon honey
- 2 tablespoons soy sauce
- 1 1/2 teaspoons wasabi powder
- 1 egg, lightly beaten
- 12 ounces canned wild salmon, drained
- 2 scallions, finely chopped
- 2 tablespoons fresh ginger, peeled, minced
- 1 teaspoon sesame oil, toasted

1. In a bowl, combine salmon with egg, ginger, scallions, and oil; mix using a fork to blend well. Form in 4 patties.
2. In a small bowl, whip wasabi powder with soy sauce and honey, until smooth.
3. Spray 4-inch rack with cooking spray. Place patties on rack and cook on High power (350 degrees F) for 10 minutes. Turn patties over and cook for an additional 5 minutes.
4. Glaze with wasabi mixture and serve.

GRILLED SALMON ON BABY ARUGULA

Arugula is a rich source of vitamin C and potassium. Salmon is a source of omega-3 fatty acids.

Servings: 2

2 (6 oz.) salmon fillets
1 1/2 tablespoons olive oil
1 1/2 tablespoons fresh lemon juice
Freshly ground black pepper, to taste
For the salad:
3 cups baby arugula leaves
2/3 cup grape or cherry tomatoes, halved
1/4 cup red onion, thinly slivered
1 tablespoon extra-virgin olive oil
1 tablespoon red-wine vinegar

1. In a bowl, marinate salmon with mixture of olive oil, lemon juice, and pepper. Let stand for at least 15 minutes.
2. Spray 4-inch rack with cooking spray. Place salmon fillets on rack and cook on High power (350 degrees F) for 4 minutes. Turn salmon over and cook for an additional 4-5 minutes.
3. Prepare salad by combining the arugula, onion, and tomatoes in a bowl. Add oil and vinegar then season with pepper. Serve at once with the fish.

BAKED HALIBUT IN GARLICKY SAUCE

A super-fast meal that is packed with the goodness of halibut and spiciness of garlic.

Servings: 4

1 (3/4 pounds) halibut fillet (1 1/2 inches thick)
Sea salt and pepper, to taste
3 garlic cloves, pressed
1/3 cup mayonnaise, whisked
2 tablespoons extra-virgin olive oil
lemon wedges, garnish

1. Lightly grease a shallow baking dish.
2. Season fish with salt and pepper and place in the prepared baking dish. Add garlic and drizzle with oil. Spread mayonnaise over the fish.
3. Place on 1-inch rack and cook on High power (350 degrees F) for 8-10 minutes or until firm and well cooked.

HAWAIIAN-STYLE SHRIMP KABOBS

A sweet and savory sauce gives these shrimp kabobs a tropical flare.

Servings: 4

2 pounds shrimp, peeled and deveined

2 cups fresh pineapple, cut into 1-inch cubes

½-pound bacon slices, cut in half

2 red bell peppers, chopped into 1 ½-inch pieces

½ pound mushrooms, stems removed

1 pint cherry tomatoes

1 cup sweet and sour sauce (like La Choy or Sweet Baby Ray's)

Wooden skewers, soaked for 20-30 minutes in water

1. Thread shrimp, pineapple, bacon, bell peppers, mushrooms, and cherry tomatoes onto skewers. Place in shallow pan. Pour sweet and sour sauce over skewers, turning to coat completely.

2. Place skewers on 4-inch rack. Cook on High Power (350 degrees F) for 6 minutes. Turn over and cook for an additional 6 minutes or until shrimp is opaque, bacon is crisp, and vegetables are tender.

LIME AND TEQUILA SHRIMP

These make a great appetizer or light summer meal.
Servings: 4

3 tablespoons lime juice
2 tablespoons tequila
¼ cup olive oil
2 cloves garlic, minced
½ teaspoon ground cumin
½ teaspoon cayenne pepper
Salt and black pepper to taste
1 pound extra-large shrimp, peeled and deveined

1. In a bowl, whisk together lime juice, tequila, olive oil, garlic, cumin, cayenne pepper, salt, and pepper. Add shrimp and marinate for 2-3 hours in refrigerator.
2. Line bottom of NuWave Oven with foil.
3. Place shrimp on 4-inch rack. Cook on High Power (350 degrees F) for 3 minutes. Flip shrimp over and cook for an additional 3 minutes or until shrimp are opaque.

SPICY CHIPOTLE SHRIMP

Servings: 4

3 cloves garlic, minced

Juice of 1 lemon

2 chipotle peppers, chopped

1 tablespoon olive oil

1 tablespoon paprika

1 teaspoon fresh cilantro, chopped

1/2 teaspoon salt

½ teaspoon ground black pepper

½ teaspoon crushed red pepper flakes

1 ½ pounds large shrimp, peeled and deveined

1. In a bowl, mix together all ingredients except for shrimp. Add shrimp and mix to coat shrimp. Marinate in refrigerator for 1 hour.
2. Line bottom of NuWave Oven with foil.
3. Remove shrimp from marinade. Place shrimp on 4-inch rack. Cook on High Power (350 degrees F) for 3 minutes. Flip shrimp over and cook for an additional 2-3 minutes, until shrimp are opaque.

ALMOND PESTO SALMON

This easy dish makes an elegant supper and is heart healthy.

Servings: 4

½ cup sliced almonds, chopped

½ cup Panko-style breadcrumbs

¾ cup basil pesto

1 ¼ pounds salmon fillets, cut into 4 pieces

Olive oil spray

1. In small bowl, combine almonds and bread crumbs.
2. Place salmon fillets on baking sheet. Spread each piece of salmon with pesto. Top with ¼ of breadcrumb mixture, pressing mixture gently into salmon. Spray lightly with olive oil.
3. Place on 3-inch rack and bake on High power (350 degrees F) for 10-12 minutes, until salmon flakes easily with fork.

CLASSIC CRAB CAKES

Easy yet elegant enough for a special occasion.
Servings: 4

2/3 cup panko breadcrumbs, divided
1 tablespoon flat-leaf parsley, chopped
2 tablespoons green onions, finely chopped
1/2 teaspoon Old Bay seasoning
1/2 teaspoon Worcestershire sauce
1/4 teaspoon sea salt
1/4 teaspoon cayenne pepper
1 teaspoon lemon juice
2 tablespoons mayonnaise
1 teaspoon Dijon mustard
1 large egg, lightly beaten
8 ounces lump crabmeat
1 lemon, quartered

1. In a large bowl, combine 1/3 cup breadcrumbs, parsley, green onions, Old Bay seasoning, Worcestershire sauce, salt, cayenne pepper, lemon juice, mayonnaise, mustard, and egg. Add crabmeat and stir until just combined.
2. Place remaining breadcrumbs in shallow dish. Form crab mixture in to 4 equal size patties. Coat each side with breadcrumbs.
3. Place foil on 3-inch rack. Spray lightly with cooking spray. Place patties on foil. Bake on High Power (350 degrees F) for 6 minutes. Turn over and cook an additional 6 minutes.

SALMON AND POTATO CAKES

A great use for leftover mashed potatoes.

Servings: 4

1 cup mashed potatoes

2 cans red salmon, drained

2 tablespoons capers, chopped

2 green onions, diced

1 egg, lightly beaten

1 tablespoon lemon juice

½ cup panko-style breadcrumbs

½ teaspoon Old Bay seasoning

Sea salt and freshly ground black pepper, to taste

1. In large bowl, mix together mashed potatoes, salmon, capers, onion, egg, lemon juice, breadcrumbs, Old Bay seasoning, salt, and pepper.
2. Form into 4 large patties or 8 small patties.
3. Spray 4-inch rack with cooking spray. Arrange patties on rack. Cook on High power (350 degrees F) for 8 minutes. Flip patties over and cook for an additional 8 minutes.

8
Vegetables and Side Dishes

ROASTED SWEET POTATO WITH ROSEMARY

Servings: 4

1 1/2 pounds sweet potatoes, scrubbed, cubed
1 teaspoon olive oil
1 dash fresh rosemary, finely chopped
1 dash lemon juice

1. In a bowl, toss sweet potatoes with oil. Evenly spread on 10-inch baking sheet, sprinkle with rosemary. Place on 1-inch rack and back on High power (350 degrees F) for 12 minutes. Flip sweet potatoes over and cook and additional 10 minutes.

2. Drizzle with lemon juice and serve.

ROASTED CARROTS WITH GARLIC AND ONION

Servings: 4

1 pound baby carrots
2-3 tablespoons extra-virgin olive oil
2-3 green onions, sliced thin
2 garlic cloves, minced
Sea salt, to taste

1. In a bowl, toss carrots with olive oil, onions, garlic, and salt. Spread carrots in single layer on parchment or foil-lined baking sheet.

2. Place on 1-inch rack and cook on High power (350 degrees F) for 15-20 minutes until carrots are tender.

TANGY ROASTED BROCCOLI WITH GARLIC

Servings: 4

1 head broccoli, cut into florets
3 cloves garlic, minced
2 teaspoons extra-virgin olive oil
1/2 teaspoon sea salt
1/2 teaspoon ground black pepper
1/2 teaspoon lemon juice

1. In a bowl, combine oil, garlic, salt, and black pepper. Add broccoli. Toss to coat. Evenly scatter broccoli on 10-inch baking sheet.
2. Place on 1-inch rack and roast on High power (350 degrees F) for about 10 minutes. Turn florets over and cook for an additional 5-7 minutes or until fork tender.
3. Plate and drizzle lemon juice. Serve at once.

Note: Broccoli stems can be used too with the florets. Double the garlic for more intense garlic flavor.

ROASTED BALSAMIC VEGETABLES

Servings: 4

1 ½ cups butternut squash, cubed
1 cup broccoli florets, chopped
½ red onion, chopped
1 zucchini, chopped
1 large garlic clove, minced
2 tablespoons olive oil
1 tablespoon balsamic vinegar
1½ teaspoon fresh rosemary
½ teaspoon sea salt

1. In a bowl, combine oil, rosemary, vinegar, salt, and pepper; mix to blend. Mix in the vegetables, mix to coat evenly.
2. Evenly spread on a parchment-lined baking sheet.
3. Place on 1-inch rack and cook on High power (350 degrees F) for about 15 minutes. Turn vegetables over and cook for an additional 15 minutes or until squash is just softened.

SWEET POTATO CASSEROLE

A crunchy pecan topping makes this feel like a decadent treat.
Servings: 6

2 cups sweet potatoes, peeled, cooked, and mashed
1/4 cup butter, melted
1 1/2 tablespoons low-fat milk
1/4 cup honey
1/4 teaspoon vanilla
1 egg, beaten
1/4 cup brown sugar
1/4 cup all-purpose flour
2 tablespoons butter
1/2 cup chopped pecans

1. Spray 8 x 8 inch baking pan with cooking spray.
2. In a large bowl, mix together sweet potatoes, melted butter, milk, honey, vanilla, and egg.
3. In a small bowl, mix together brown sugar and flour. Cut in 3 tablespoons butter until mixture is crumbly. Add pecans and stir.
4. Sprinkle pecan mixture over sweet potatoes.
5. Place on 1-inch rack and cook for 25-30 minutes on 350 degrees F (High) or until golden brown.

KALE CHIPS

Next time you are craving potato chips, reach for these low-cal snacks instead.

Servings: 6

1 large bunch kale
1 tablespoon olive oil
1/4 teaspoon sea salt

1. Line cookie sheet with parchment paper.
2. Cut stems from kale. Wash and thoroughly dry kale leaves. (Hint: Use a salad spinner)
3. Spread kale out on baking sheet in single layer. Drizzle with olive oil and season with salt.
4. Place on 1-inch rack and cook 3-5 minutes, depending on how crispy you like your kale chips.

BAKED MACARONI AND CHEESE

Servings: 6-8

1 (1 pound) box elbow macaroni
1 pound extra-sharp cheddar cheese, shredded
4 tablespoons butter, cut into pieces
2 eggs, beaten
1 (12 ounce) can evaporated milk
1 teaspoon Dijon mustard
Salt and freshly ground black pepper, to taste
½ cup bread crumbs (Panko-style preferred)

1. Cook macaroni according to package directions.
2. Spray casserole dish with cooking spray.
3. Add all ingredients except for bread crumbs to casserole dish and mix well to combine. Sprinkle with bread crumbs.
4. Cover with foil and place pan on 1-inch rack. Bake on High (350 degrees F) for 15-20 minutes. Remove foil and cook for an additional 5-10 minutes or until golden brown.

SPINACH AND KALE BALLS WITH HERBS

Spinach contains many antioxidants and helps protect against inflammation, while kale promotes the detoxification process.

Servings: 6

- 1 cup (8 ounces) frozen spinach, thawed and chopped
- 1/2 cup onion, finely chopped
- 3 tbsp. and 1 tsp. olive oil
- 1 large egg, beaten
- 1 cup (8 ounces) frozen kale, thawed and drained
- 1/4 tsp. garlic powder
- 1/4 tsp. ground thyme
- 1/4 tsp. dried sage, rubbed
- 1/4 tsp. dried rosemary
- 1/2 cup dry seasoned bread crumbs
- 1/4 cup Parmesan cheese, grated
- 1/4 tsp. dried oregano
- 1 pinch ground black pepper

1. Line baking sheet with parchment paper.
2. In a mixing bowl, whisk olive oil and eggs; add in spinach and onions, toss to coat. Add in the rest of the ingredients, mix to blend. Form 1 1/2-inch balls and arrange 1-inch apart on the lined baking sheet.
3. Place in oven on 1-inch rack and cook on High power (350 degrees F) for 12 minutes. Take out sheet and flip balls over. Return and continue cooking for another 10-12 minutes more or until golden brown.
4. Serve with yogurt dip, if desired.

CURRIED ZUCCHINI CHIPS

Servings: 2

1 medium zucchini, thinly sliced
1 tablespoon olive oil
¼ teaspoon curry powder
⅛ teaspoon garlic powder
⅛ teaspoon salt

1. Lightly grease paper-lined baking sheet.
2. Arrange zucchini slices in single layer on the prepared baking sheet. Drizzle olive oil and sprinkle with curry powder, garlic powder, and salt.
3. Place baking sheet on 1-inch rack and bake on High power (350 degrees F) for 12 minutes. Flip zucchini over and cook for an additional 10 minutes or until very crisp. Cool and store in an airtight container

ROASTED CHICKPEAS

The texture of roasted chickpeas is crispy and crunch and is a perfect snack when you're craving a salty treat.

Servings: 4

2 cans (15-ounce) chickpeas
3 tablespoons olive oil
Sea salt, to taste
Spice of choice (try cayenne pepper, turmeric, cumin)

1. Drain chickpeas and place in strainer. Rinse with cold running water for several seconds. Shake to remove excess water. Lay out several paper towels and spread chickpeas over them. Top with another layer of paper towels and press gently to absorb water.

2. Spread chickpeas on 10 x 10 baking sheet. Drizzle with olive oil. Mix using large spoon or spatula to coat chickpeas evenly. Sprinkle with salt and spices.

3. Place pan on 1-inch rack and roast on High power (350 degrees F) 15 minutes. Turn chickpeas and cook an additional 10-12 minutes or until chickpeas are golden brown and crunchy.

4. Check seasoning and add additional salt and spices to taste.

ROASTED PEPPERS

Serves: 4

4 peppers
1 tablespoon olive oil

1. Wash, core, and halve peppers. Remove seeds and pith.
2. Place pepper halves in baking pan skin side up.
3. Brush olive oil on pepper halves.
4. Place pan on 4-inch rack.
5. Cook on High power (350 degrees F) 15 minutes or until skins blister and blacken.
6. Turn peppers over and cook an additional 10 minutes or until pepper skins are evenly roasted.
7. Allow peppers to cool in pan in covered NuWave oven for about 30 minutes.
8. Remove peppers from oven and place on cutting board. Peel off skins, scraping off any remaining skin with knife.

ROASTED BEETS AND FENNEL WITH BALSAMIC GLAZE

Servings: 4

3-4 large beets, peeled and cut into chunks
1 stalk fennel, tops cut off and cut into chunks
1 medium onion, diced
1/3 cup extra virgin olive oil
1/3 cup balsamic vinegar
Sea salt, to taste

1. Spread beets, fennel, and onion in single layer on baking sheet.
2. Drizzle olive oil and then vinegar over vegetables. Season with salt. Mix with spoon until vegetables are thoroughly coated.
3. Place on 1-inch rack in NuWave Oven and cook on High Power (350 degrees F) for 40-50 minutes or until beets are tender. Turn vegetables every 15 minutes or so while cooking.

FRUIT AND VEGETABLE SKEWERS

A fresh and healthy dinner that is sure to please.
Servings: 4

¼ cup olive oil

3 tablespoons lemon juice

1 clove garlic, minced

2 tablespoons parsley, chopped

½ teaspoon salt

½ teaspoon ground black pepper

1 zucchini, cut into slices

1 yellow squash, cut into slices

½ red bell pepper, cut into ½-inch pieces

½ cup cherry tomatoes

½ cup fresh pineapple chunks

4 wooden skewers, soaked for 20-30 minutes in water

1. Mix olive oil, lemon juice, garlic, parsley, salt, and pepper in a bowl. Pour into large resealable plastic bag. Add zucchini, squash, bell pepper, and tomatoes. Seal bag, shake to coat vegetables, and place in refrigerator for a minimum of 1 hour.

2. Remove vegetables from marinade and thread onto skewers, along with pineapple, alternating among each item.

3. Line bottom of NuWave Oven with foil for easier clean-up.

4. Place skewers on 4-inch rack. Cook on High Power (350 degrees F) for 8 minutes. Turn skewers over and cook for an additional 6-8 minutes until veggies are desired level of doneness.

5. Remove from NuWave Oven, transfer to plate, and serve.

BAKED PARMESAN POTATO WEDGES

These are delicious as an appetizer or side dish.
Servings: 4

3 large potatoes (Russet)
3 tablespoons olive oil
1 ½ teaspoons salt
2 teaspoons garlic powder
2 teaspoons Italian seasoning
½ cup shredded Parmesan cheese

1. Slice potatoes into wedges and place in large bowl. Drizzle with olive oil, mix to coat. Sprinkle potatoes with salt, garlic powder, and Italian seasoning, mixing to coat. Sprinkle with Parmesan cheese, mix to coat.
2. Spread potatoes in single layer on lightly greased baking sheet.
3. Place on 1-inch rack and bake for 20-25 minutes on High power (350 degrees F) until potatoes are tender and golden brown.
4. Serve with ranch or blue cheese dressing for dipping.

BAKED POTATO NACHOS

These make a delicious snack to serve while watching the big game!

Servings: 4

4 medium potatoes, washed and sliced into ¼-thich round slices
1 tablespoon olive oil
Sea salt and ground black pepper, to taste
4 strips bacon, cooked
½ cup shredded Monterey cheese
½ cup shredded cheddar cheese
Sour cream, for serving

1. Lightly spray baking pan with cooking spray.
2. Place potato slices in pot, cover with water, and bring to boil. Cook for 3 minutes until just tender.
3. Drain potatoes and pat dry. Place potatoes on baking sheet. Brush with olive oil and season with salt and pepper.
4. Crumble bacon strips onto potatoes. Top with cheeses.
5. Place pan on 1-inch rack and cook on High Power (350 degrees F) for 8-10 minutes, until cheese is melted and light golden brown.
6. Serve with sour cream.

GREEK-STYLE POTATOES

Servings: 4

4 large white potatoes
Juice of 1 lemon
2 tablespoons olive oil
Sea salt and ground black pepper, to taste
1 teaspoon oregano
3 cloves garlic, minced
½ teaspoon paprika
¾ cup chicken broth
Fresh parsley, chopped, for garnish

1. Cut potatoes in half, and then each half into quarters (if potatoes are very large, cut each piece in half again, each slice should be about an inch wide). Place potatoes in large bowl.

2. Add lemon juice, olive oil, salt, pepper, oregano, garlic, and paprika to bowl. Mix well to coat potatoes.

3. Place potatoes into baking dish. Pour chicken broth over potatoes. Cover with foil.

4. Place pan on 1-inch rack and bake on High Power (350 degrees F) for 20-25 minutes until potatoes are tender.

5. Sprinkle with fresh parsley and serve.

BAKED PARMESAN ZUCCHINI WEDGES

These healthy zucchini wedges are positively addictive.

Servings: 4

4 zucchini, cut in half and then quartered lengthwise
2 tablespoons olive oil
½ teaspoon oregano
½ teaspoon basil
½ teaspoon thyme
½ teaspoon garlic powder
1 teaspoon sea salt
1 teaspoon ground black pepper
½ cup shredded Parmesan cheese

1. Place zucchini wedges into large bowl. Drizzle with olive oil and toss to coat.

2. In small bowl, mix together oregano, basil, thyme, garlic powder, salt, and black pepper. Sprinkle mixture over zucchini wedges and toss to coat. Sprinkle with Parmesan cheese and toss to coat.

3. Spread zucchini wedges in single layer on lightly greased baking sheet.

4. Place on 1-inch rack and cook on High power (350 degrees F) for 8 minutes. Turn zucchini over and cook for an additional 7-8 minutes, or until zucchini is golden brown.

5. Remove from NuWave Oven and serve immediately with ranch or blue cheese dressing for dipping.

CHEESY BACON TOPPED POTATO FRIES

Servings: 4

Cooking spray
2 large russet potatoes, washed and cut into 1/8-inch thick rounds
Sea salt and freshly ground black pepper, to taste
1 cup Colby jack or cheddar cheese, shredded
½ cup bacon crumbles
Chopped parsley, for garnish

1. Lightly spray 10-inch baking sheet with cooking spray. Lay potato slices on pan, overlapping as needed. Season with salt and pepper. Sprinkle cheese evenly over potatoes and then top with bacon crumbles.

2. Place pan on 1-inch rack and cook on High power (350 degrees F) for 35-40 minutes until potatoes are tender.

OVEN-ROASTED CORN ON THE COB

This is my absolute favorite way to cook corn.

Servings: 4

4 ears corn, husks removed
4 tablespoons butter, room temperature
Sea salt and freshly ground black pepper, to taste
1 teaspoon cayenne pepper

1. Spread butter on ears of corn. Season with salt, black pepper, and cayenne pepper. Wrap corn in foil.

2. Place on 4-inch rack and cook on High power (350 degrees F) for 5 minutes, roll corn over and cook for an additional 5 minutes.

OVEN-ROASTED GARLICKY CAULIFLOWER

Servings: 3-4

½ large head cauliflower, separated into florets
4 cloves garlic, minced
1 ½ tablespoons olive oil
Sea salt and freshly ground black pepper, to taste
¼ cup Parmesan cheese
1 tablespoon fresh parsley, chopped

1. Place cauliflower florets into large bowl. Add garlic and olive oil and stir to coat cauliflower. Season with salt and pepper.
2. Spread cauliflower onto liner pan. Top with Parmesan cheese and parsley.
3. Place on 1-inch rack and roast on High power (350 degrees F) for 20-25 minutes. Remove from oven at once.

9
Desserts and Baked Goods

Didn't know you could make baked goods in the your NuWave Oven? Well you can!

LEMON-ZUCCHINI MUFFINS

These muffins are a great way to sneak in an extra serving of vegetables.
Servings: 12 muffins (make in two batches)

2 cups all-purpose flour
1/2 cup sugar
1 tablespoon baking powder
1/4 teaspoon salt
1/4 teaspoon cinnamon
1/4 teaspoon nutmeg
1 cup shredded zucchini
3/4 cup nonfat milk
2 tablespoons olive oil
2 tablespoons lemon juice
1 egg
Nonstick cooking spray

1. Prepare 6-muffin tin by spraying lightly with cooking spray or lining with muffin liners.
2. In a mixing bowl, combine flour, sugar, baking powder, salt, cinnamon, and nutmeg.
3. In a separate bowl, combine zucchini, milk, oil, lemon juice, and egg. Stir well.
4. Add zucchini mixture to flour mixture. Stir until just combined. Do not over stir.
5. Pour batter into prepared muffin cups. Place pan on 1-inch rack and bake for 20 minutes at 350 degrees (High) or until light golden brown.

BAKED STUFFED APPLES

Perfect for dessert on a crisp autumn day.
Servings: 4

4 large apples (Honeycrisp, Fuji, Rome)
1/4 cup coconut flakes
1/4 cup dried cranberries or apricots
2 teaspoons orange zest, grated
1/2 cup orange juice
2 tablespoons brown sugar

1. Cut top off apple and hollow out center with knife or apple corer. Arrange in non-stick baking pan.
2. In a bowl, combine coconut, cranberries, and orange zest. Divide evenly and fill centers of apples.
3. In a bowl, mix orange juice and brown sugar. Pour over apples.
4. Place pan on 1-inch rack and cook 5-6 minutes until apples are tender.
5. Serve warm.

BROILED PEACHES WITH HONEY

Servings: 4

2 peaches
1 tablespoon extra-virgin olive oil
1 tablespoon honey

1. Cut peaches in half and remove pits. Brush cut side of peaches with olive oil.
2. Place on parchment-lined pan and place on 4-inch rack. Cook in NuWave Oven on High power (350 degrees F) for 5-6 minutes or until peaches are golden brown and caramelized.
3. Drizzle with honey and serve.

CARROT CAKE COOKIES

These cookies are full of carrot cake flavor in every bit.
Servings: 24 cookies

1/4 cup packed light-brown sugar
1/4 cup sugar
1/4 cup oil
1/4 cup applesauce or fruit puree
1 eggs
1/2 teaspoon vanilla
1/2 cup flour
1/2 cup whole wheat flour
1/2 teaspoon baking soda
1/2 teaspoon baking powder
1/8 teaspoon salt
1/2 teaspoon ground cinnamon
1/4 teaspoon ground nutmeg
1/4 teaspoon ground ginger
1 cups old-fashioned rolled oats (raw)
3/4 cup finely grated carrots (about 2 carrots)
1/2 cup raisins or golden raisins

1. Mix together sugars, oil, applesauce, egg, and vanilla.
2. In a separate bowl, mix together all dry ingredients.
3. Add dry ingredients into wet ingredients. Mix until just blended. Stir in carrots and raisins.
4. Drop by teaspoonful onto silicone baking ring or parchment-lined cookie sheet.
5. Place on 1-inch rack and cook at 300 degrees F (Level 8) for 12-14 minutes or until golden brown.

OATMEAL WALNUT CHOCOLATE CHIP COOKIES

We've reduced the amount of saturated fat in these cookies without sacrificing any of the taste.

Servings: 24 cookies

1 cup rolled oats (not quick-cooking)
1/4 cup all-purpose flour
1/4 cup whole-wheat pastry flour
1/2 teaspoon ground cinnamon
1/4 teaspoon baking soda
1/4 teaspoon salt
1/4 cup tahini (sesame seed paste)
4 tablespoons cold unsalted butter, cut into pieces
1/3 cup granulated sugar
1/3 cup packed light brown sugar
1 large egg
1/2 tablespoon vanilla extract
1/2 cup semisweet or bittersweet chocolate chips
1/4 cup chopped walnuts

1. Mix together oats, flour, cinnamon, baking soda, and salt in bowl.

2. In another large bowl, whisk together tahini, butter, sugar, brown sugar, egg, and vanilla until smooth.

3. Add in oat mixture and mix until just moistened.

4. Stir in chocolate chips and walnuts.

5. Place tablespoon-size portions of batter onto silicone baking ring or parchment-lined cookie sheet.

6. Put on 1-inch rack and cook at 350 degrees F (High) for 14-16 minutes or until cookies are golden brown.

Note: Tahini can be substituted with almond butter or other nut butter.

BAKED APPLES WITH WALNUTS, HONEY, AND CINNAMON

These cinnamon apples are perfect on a cool autumn day.

Servings: 4

1 teaspoon cinnamon
1/4 cup honey
4 ounces walnuts, coarsely chopped
4 large apples
1/2 tablespoon lemon juice

1. In a mixing bowl, mix together cinnamon, honey, and walnuts.
2. Core apples, scoop out enough of the insides to make room for nut stuffing. Place apples in 10-inch baking dish.
3. Spoon nut filling into each apple. Drizzle a little lemon juice on top of each apple.
4. Place pan on 3- or 4-inch rack and cook on High power (400 degrees F for Elite) for 12-15 minutes or until apples are tender.
5. Remove from NuWave Oven and let cool.

DEHYDRATED CINNAMON APPLE CHIPS

These will make your house smell like apple pie.

Servings: 4

3 to 4 large apples (gala, red delicious, or granny smith are all good options)
1 tablespoon ground cinnamon
1 tablespoon brown sugar (optional)

1. Slice off top side (stem) of apples and then slice apples into rounds around 1/8-inch to ¼-inch thick. This is easiest with a mandolin slicer but can also be done with a sharp knife.
2. Place apple slices in bowl and sprinkle with cinnamon and sugar. Toss gently to coat.
3. Spray 4-inch rack with cooking spray. Arrange apple slices on rack. (Note: You can use both racks to increase cooking area.) Prop dome open using dome holder to allow steam to escape during dehydration.
4. Cook on Power level 3 (150 degrees F) for 4 hours.
5. Remove from NuWave oven immediately. Allow to cool before serving.

DEHYDRATED BANANA AND STRAWBERRY CHIPS

These two fruits just taste great together.

Servings: 4

2 bananas
20 strawberries

1. Peel bananas and slice into rounds about ¼-inch thick. Wash strawberries and pat dry with paper towel. Cut strawberries into slices about ¼-inch thick.
2. Arrange banana and strawberry slices onto racks. Prop side of dome open using dome holder to allow steam to escape.
3. Cook on Power level 3 (150 degrees F) for 3 ½ to 4 hours.
4. Remove from NuWave Oven immediately. Let cool before eating.

CRANBERRY BARS

These bars are both tart and sweet.

Servings: 12

1 ½ cups whole cranberries
¾ cup white sugar
¾ cup water
1 package yellow cake mix
6 tablespoons butter, melted
2 eggs
¾ cup rolled oats
½ cup brown sugar
1 teaspoon ginger
1 teaspoon cinnamon

1. Spray 8 x 8 baking pan with cooking spray.
2. Add cranberries, sugar, and water to saucepan. Cook over medium heat, stirring occasionally, until all cranberries have popped and mixture has thickened (10-15 minutes). Remove from heat and let cool.
3. In a large bowl, mix together cake mix, butter, eggs, oats, brown sugar, ginger, and cinnamon. Spread 2/3 of mixture into baking pan. Use back of spoon to press down evenly to form crust. Spread cranberry mixture evenly over crust. Top with remaining mixture.
4. Place on 1-inch rack and bake on Power level High (350 degrees F) for 30-35 minutes, until top is lightly browned. Allow to cool before cutting.

HONEY CORNBREAD

This sweet cornbread will melt in your mouth.

Servings: 8

1 cup all-purpose flour
1 cup yellow cornmeal
¼ cup white sugar
1 tablespoon baking powder
1 cup heavy cream
¼ cup vegetable oil
¼ cup honey
2 eggs, lightly beaten

1. Lightly grease 10 x 10 baking pan.
2. In a large mixing bowl, stir together flour, cornmeal, sugar, and baking powder. Add in cream, oil, honey, and eggs. Stir to combine.
3. Pour into baking pan. Bake on 1-inch rack on Power Level High (350 degrees F) for 20 minutes. Let rest for 1-2 minutes before removing from NuWave Oven.

CHOCOLATE ZUCCHINI BREAD

This moist zucchini bread is great way to sneak a few extra vegetables in.

Servings: 2 loaves

3 eggs
2 cup white sugar
1/3 cup cocoa powder
1 cup vegetable oil
2 cups zucchini, grated
1 teaspoon vanilla extract
2 cups all-purpose flour
1 teaspoon baking soda
1 teaspoon salt
1 teaspoon cinnamon
¾ cup semisweet chocolate chips

1. Spray two 9 x 5-inch loaf pans with cooking spray.
2. In a large mixing bowl, combine eggs, sugar, cocoa powder, oil, grated zucchini, and vanilla. Beat well. Stir in flour, baking soda, salt, and cinnamon. Stir in chocolate chips.
3. Pour batter into prepared pans. Bake on 1-inch rack on Power level High (350 degrees F) for 40-45 minutes until knife inserted in center comes out clean. Let bread rest inside dome for 1-2 minutes before removing from NuWave Oven. Allow to cool before slicing.

PINEAPPLE BANANA NUT BREAD

Servings: 2 loaves

3 cups all-purpose flour
¾ teaspoon salt
1 teaspoon baking soda
2 cups white sugar
1 teaspoon ground cinnamon
1 cup walnuts, chopped
3 eggs, lightly beaten
1 cup vegetable oil
4 ripe bananas, mashed
1 (8 ounce) can crushed pineapple, drained
2 teaspoons vanilla extract

1. Spray two 9 x 5-inch loaf pans with cooking spray.
2. In large mixing bowl, combine flour, salt, baking soda, sugar, and cinnamon. Add in walnuts, eggs, oil, banana, pineapple, and vanilla. Stir until just blended. Pour batter into pans.
3. Place pans on 1-inch rack and bake on High power (350 degrees F) for 45-50 minutes or until toothpick inserted in center comes out clean. Let rest under dome for 1-2 minutes before removing from NuWave Oven. Cool before slicing.

BLUEBERRY LEMON POUND CAKE

This cake is perfect to make in the summer when blueberries are abundant.

Servings: 1 cake

2 sticks butter, unsalted, softened
1 cup white sugar
1 teaspoon baking powder
¼ cup lemon juice
2 tablespoons lemon zest
1 teaspoon vanilla extract
1/8 teaspoon salt
4 eggs
2 cups all-purpose flour
1 ½ cups fresh blueberries

1. Spray 9 x 5 loaf pan with cooking spray.
2. Beat together butter, sugar, and baking powder until smooth and fluffy. Add lemon juice, lemon zest, vanilla, and salt. Mix until combined. Add eggs, one at a time, beating until smooth after each. Add flour and mix until just combined. Fold in blueberries.
3. Spread batter into pan. Shake pan to even out batter.
4. Place Extender Ring on base. Place pan on 1-inch rack and cook on Power Level 9 (325 degrees F) for 45-50 minutes or until knife inserted in center comes out clean.
5. Remove from NuWave Oven and allow to cool before slicing.

Internal Meat and Poultry Temperature Guide

MEAT	FAHRENHEIT	CELSIUS
BEEF:		
Rare	120°F to 125°F	45°C to 50°C
Medium-Rare	130°F to 135°F	55°C to 60°C
Medium	140°F to 145°F	60°C to 65°C
Medium-Well	150°F to 155°F	65°C to 70°C
Well Done	160°F and above	70°C and above
LAMB:		
Rare	135°F	60°C
Medium-rare	140°F to 150°F	60°C to 65°C
Medium	160°F	70°C
Well done	165°F and above	75°C and above
POULTRY:		
Chicken	165°F to 175°F	75°C to 80°C
Turkey	165°F to 175°F	75°C to 80°C
PORK:		
Fresh Pork	145°F	63°C
Ham (Fully-Cooked)	140°F	60°C
Ham (Uncooked)	145°F	63°C

From the Author

Thank you for reading the *NuWave Oven Cookbook: Complete Guide to Making the Most of Your NuWave Oven*. I sincerely hope that you found this book informative and helpful and that it helps you to create delicious foods for yourself, family, and friends.

Happy cooking!

Index

A

Almond Pesto Salmon 137
appetizers
    Asparagus Wrapped in Bacon 26
    Avocado Wrapped in Bacon 25
    Bacon-Wrapped Jalapeno Poppers 30
    Spinach and Sun-Dried Tomato Stuffed Mushrooms 32
    Sweet and Spicy Nuts 29
apples
    Apple Butter Pork Tenderloin 82
    Apple-Stuffed Chicken Breast 69
    Baked Apples with Walnuts, Honey, and Cinnamon 180
    Baked Stuffed Apples 174
    Dehydrated Cinnamon Apple Chips 183
Artichoke Grilled Cheese Sandwich 35
asparagus
    Asparagus Wrapped in Bacon 26
    Grilled Salmon and Asparagus with Lemon Butter 116
    Spring Frittata with Smoked Salmon and Asparagus 16
avocado
    Avocado Wrapped in Bacon 25
    Grilled Cheese with Avocado and Tomato 36
    Grilled Chicken Salad with Mango and Avocado 63

B

Bacon 7
    Asparagus Wrapped in Bacon 26
    Avocado Wrapped in Bacon 25
    Bacon and Chicken Kabobs 60
    Bacon-Wrapped Jalapeno Poppers 30
    Bacon-Wrapped Pork Medallions 86
    Bacon-Wrappted Chicken with Potatoes 65
    Baked Fish with Herbed Bacon 119
    Candied Bacon Jerky 87
    Cheesy Bacon Topped Potato Fries 166
    Egg and Bacon Breakfast Muffins 8
    Ham, Cheese, and Bacon Quiche 15
Baked Apples with Walnuts, Honey, and Cinnamon 180
Baked Fish with Herbed Bacon 119
baked goods
    Blueberry Lemon Pound Cake 192
    Carrot Cake Cookies 177
    Chocolate Zucchini Bread 188
    Cranberry Bars 185
    Honey Cornbread 187
    Lemon-Zucchini Muffins 172
    Oatmeal Walnut Chocolate Chip Cookies 179
    Pineapple Banana Nut Bread 191
Baked Greek Omelet with Tomatoes and Feta 12
Baked Halibut in Garlicky Sauce 130
Baked Macaroni and Cheese 150
Baked Parmesan Potato Wedges 159
Baked Parmesan Zucchini Wedges 165
Baked Potato Nachos 161
Baked-Stuffed Apples 174
banana
    Dehydrated Banana and Strawberry Chips 184
    Pineapple Banana Nut Bread 191
Barbecue Ribs 90
beef
    Beef and Veggie Kabobs with Spicy Mediterraean Marinade 101
    Beef Roast 104
    French Onion Meatloaf 100
    Grilled Steak with Ginger Marinade 103
    Gruyere Mushroom Burgers 105
    Spicy Beef Jerky 111
    Yummy Homestyle Meatloaf 99
beets
    Roasted Beets and Fennel with Balsamic Glaze 157
blueberries
    Blueberry Lemon Pound Cake 192
    Overnight Baked Blueberry and Cream Cheese French Toast 20
breakfast. See also eggs
    Bacon 7
    Baked Eggs with Spinach and Tomatoes 13
    Baked Greek Omelet with Tomatoes and Feta 12
    Egg and Bacon Breakfast Muffins 8
    Healthy Low-Fat Granola 11
    Overnight Baked Blueberry and Cream Cheese French Toast 20
broccoli
    Chicken, Broccoli, and Rice Bake 47
    Roasted Balsamic Vegetables 146
    Tangy Roasted Broccoli with Garlic 145
Broiled Peaches with Honey 175
burgers
    Gruyere Mushroom Burgers 105
    Southwest-Style Turkey Burgers 71
    Wasabi Salmon Burgers 127

C

Candied Bacon Jerky 87
carrots
   Carrot Cake Cookies 177
   Roasted Carrots with Garlic and Onion 143
cauliflower
   Oven-Roasted Garlicky Cauliflower 169
Cheesy Bacon Topped Potato Fries 166
chicken
   Apple-Stuffed Chicken Breast 69
   Bacon and Chicken Kabobs 60
   Bacon-Wrapped Chicken with Potatoes 65
   Chicken, Broccoli, and Rice Bake 47
   Chicken Enchilada Bake 44
   Creamy Chicken and Cheese Bake 41
   Crunchy-Spicy Baked Chicken Drumsticks 51
   Garlic Ginger Chicken Wings 56
   Grilled Chicken Salad with Mango and Avocado 63
   Hot and Spicy Baked Buffalo Chicken Wings 54
   Jerk Chicken Wings 59
   Juicy Whole Roasted Chicken 64
   Just Like KFC NuWave Oven-Fried Chicken 52
   Mediterranean Lemon Chicken and Potatoes 40
   NuWave Thai Coconut Chicken 67
   Oven Fried Chicken Wings 57
   Pesto Chicken with Prosciutto and Gouda 68
   Spicy Chili Chicken Breasts 42
   Tandoori Chicken Skewers 43
   Teriyaki Wings 48
chickpeas
   Roasted Chickpeas 154
Chinese-Style Barbecued Pork 93
Chocolate Zucchini Bread 188
Citrus Baked Salmon 124
Classic Crab Cakes 138
cod
   Baked Fish with Herbed Bacon 119
   Fish Baked with Tomatoes and Potatoes 120
   Panko-Crusted Cod 115
conduction 2
convection 2
cookies
   Carrot Cake Cookies 177
   Oatmeal Walnut Chocolate Chip Cookies 179
cooking times 3
cookware 3
corn
   Oven-Roasted Corn on the Cob 167
cornbread
   Honey Cornbread 187
crab
   Classic Crab Cakes 138
   Crab Quiche 22

Cranberry Bars 185
Creamy Chicken and Cheese Bake 41
Crunchy-Spicy Baked Chicken Drumsticks 51
Cuban-Style Pork Loin 76
Curried Zucchini Chips 153

D

Dehydrated Banana and Strawberry Chips 184
Dehydrated Cinnamon Apple Chips 183
dehydrating 3

E

Easy Peasy Ham and Cheese Casserole 80
Easy, Tasty Lamb Chops 107
eggs
   Baked Eggs with Spinach and Tomatoes 13
   Baked Greek Omelet with Tomatoes and Feta 12
   Crab Quiche 22
   Egg and Bacon Breakfast Muffins 8
   Ham, Cheese, and Bacon Quiche 15
   Spring Frittata with Smoked Salmon and Asparagus 16
   Sun-Dried Tomato and Goat Cheese Frittata with Basil 19
enchiladas
   Chicken Enchilada Bake 44
energy efficiency 1
Extender Ring 3

F

fennel
   Roasted Beets and Fennel with Balsamic Glaze 157
fish. See also seafood
   Almond Pesto Salmon 137
   Baked Fish with Herbed Bacon 119
   Baked Halibut in Garlicky Sauce 130
   Citrus Baked Salmon 124
   Fish Baked with Tomatoes and Potatoes 120
   Grilled Salmon and Asparagus with Lemon Butter 116
   Grilled Salmon on Baby Arugula 128
   Open-Faced Tuna Melt 33
   Orange Marmalade Marinated Salmon 118
   Panko-Crusted Cod 115
   Soy and Ginger Mahi Mahi 123
   Wasabi Salmon Burgers 127
French Onion Meatloaf 100
French toast
   Overnight Baked Blueberry and Cream Cheese French Toast 20
frequently asked questions (FAQs) 3
frittata
   Spring Frittata with Smoked Salmon and Asparagus 16
   Sun-Dried Tomato and Goat Cheese Frittata with Basil 19
frozen food 3
Fruit and Vegetable Skewers 158

G

Garlic Ginger Chicken Wings 56
Glazed Pork Chops with Apricot-Mango Salsa 85
granola 11
Greek-Style Lamb Kabobs 108
Greek-Style Potatoes 162
Grilled Chicken Salad with Mango and Avocado 63
Grilled Salmon and Asparagus with Lemon Butter 116
Grilled Salmon on Baby Arugula 128
Grilled Steak with Ginger Marinade 103
Gruyere Mushroom Burgers 105

H

halibut
   Baked Halibut in Garlicky Sauce 130
halogen ovens 2
ham
   Easy Peasy Ham and Cheese Casserole 80
   Ham, Cheese, and Bacon Quiche 15
Hawaiian-Style Shrimp Kabobs 131
Healthy Low-Fat Granola 11
Herb-Roasted Turkey Breast 72
Honey Cornbread 187
Honey-Ginger Pork Chops 79
Hot and Spicy Baked Buffalo Chicken Wings 54

I

infrared heat 2
internal meat and poultry temperature guide 195
Italian Sausage Casserole 77

J

jalapeno peppers
   Bacon-Wrapped Jalapeno Poppers 30
Jerk Chicken Wings 59
Juicy Whole Roasted Chicken 64
Just Like KFC NuWave Oven-Fried Chicken 52

K

kale
   Kale Chips 149
   Spinach and Kale Balls with Herbs 151

L

lamb
   Easy, Tasty Lamb Chops 107
   Greek-Style Lamb Kabobs 108
Lemon-Zucchini Muffins 172
Lime and Tequila Shrimp 133

M

mahi mahi
   Soy and Ginger Mahi Mahi 123
mango
   Glazed Pork Chops with Apricot-Mango Salsa 85
   Grilled Chicken Salad with Mango and Avocado 63
meatloaf
   French Onion Meatloaf 100
   Yummy Homestyle Meatloaf 99
Mediterranean Lemon Chicken and Potatoes 40
muffins
   Egg and Bacon Breakfast Muffins 8
   Lemon-Zucchini Muffins 172
mushrooms
   Gruyere Mushroom Burgers 105
   Spinach and Sun-Dried Tomato Stuffed Mushrooms 32

N

nuts
   Sweet and Spicy Nuts 29
NuWave Oven
  advantages of 1
  cleaning 3
  FAQs 3
  racks 3
  science of 2
  temperature conversion guide 4
  tips and tricks for 2
  vs. halogen oven 2
NuWave Thai Coconut Chicken 67

O

Oatmeal Walnut Chocolate Chip Cookies 179
omelette
   Baked Greek Omelet with Tomatoes and Feta 12
Open-Faced Tuna Melt 33
Orange Marmalade Marinated Salmon 118
Oven Fried Chicken Wings 57
Oven-Roasted Corn on the Cob 167
Oven-Roasted Garlicky Cauliflower 169
Overnight Baked Blueberry and Cream Cheese French Toast 20

P

Panko-Crusted Cod 115
Parmesan-Crusted Pork Chops 94
peaches
   Broiled Peaches with Honey 175
peppers
   Fruit and Vegetable Skewers 158
   Roasted Peppers 156
Pesto Chicken with Prosciutto and Gouda 68
Pineapple Banana Nut Bread 191
pork

Apple Butter Pork Tenderloin 82
Bacon 7
Bacon-Wrapped Pork Medallions 86
Barbecue Ribs 90
Chinese-Style Barbecued Pork 93
Cuban-Style Pork Loin 76
Easy Peasy Ham and Cheese Casserole 80
Glazed Pork Chops with Apricot-Mango Salsa 85
Honey-Ginger Pork Chops 79
Italian Sausage Casserole 77
Parmesan-Crusted Pork Chops 94
Teriyaki Pork Kabobs 89

potatoes
   Bacon-Wrapped Chicken with Potatoes 65
   Baked Parmesan Potato Wedges 159
   Baked Potato Nachos 161
   Cheesy Bacon Topped Potato Fries 166
   Fish Baked with Tomatoes and Potatoes 120
   Greek-Style Potatoes 162
   Mediterranean Lemon Chicken and Potatoes 40
   Salmon and Potato Cakes 139

Q

quiche
   Crab Quiche 22
   Ham, Cheese, and Bacon Quiche 15

R

ribs
   Barbecue Ribs 90
Roasted Balsamic Vegetables 146
Roasted Beets and Fennel with Balsamic Glaze 157
Roasted Carrots with Garlic and Onion 143
Roasted Chickpeas 154
Roasted Peppers 156
Roasted Sweet Potato with Rosemary 142

S

salad
   Grilled Chicken Salad with Mango and Avocado 63
salmon
   Almond Pesto Salmon 137
   Citrus Baked Salmon 124
   Grilled Salmon and Asparagus with Lemon Butter 116
   Grilled Salmon on Baby Arugula 128
   Orange Marmalade Marinated Salmon 118
   Salmon and Potato Cakes 139
   Spring Frittata with Smoked Salmon and Asparagus 16
   Wasabi Salmon Burgers 127
sandwiches
   Artichoke Grilled Cheese Sandwich 35
   Grilled Cheese with Avocado and Tomato 36
   Open-Faced Tuna Melt 33

sausage
   Italian Sausage Casserole 77
seafood. See also fish
   Classic Crab Cakes 138
   Crab Quiche 22
   Hawaiian-Style Shrimp Kabobs 131
   Salmon and Potato Cakes 139
   Spicy Chipotle Shrimp 134
shrimp
   Hawaiian-Style Shrimp Kabobs 131
   Lime and Tequila Shrimp 133
   Spicy Chipotle Shrimp 134
Southwest-Style Turkey Burgers 71
Soy and Ginger Mahi Mahi 123
Spicy Beef Jerky 111
Spicy Chili Chicken Breasts 42
Spicy Chipotle Shrimp 134
spinach
   Baked Eggs with Spinach and Tomatoes 13
   Baked Greek Omelet with Tomatoes and Feta 12
   Spinach and Kale Balls with Herbs 151
   Spinach and Sun-Dried Tomato Stuffed Mushrooms 32
Spring Frittata with Smoked Salmon and Asparagus 16
squash
   Fruit and Vegetable Skewers 158
   Roasted Balsamic Vegetables 146
steaming 3
strawberries
   Dehydrated Banana and Strawberry Chips 184
sun-dried tomatoes
   Spinach and Sun-Dried Tomato Stuffed Mushrooms 32
   Sun-Dried Tomato and Goat Cheese Frittata with Basil 19
Sweet and Spicy Nuts 29
sweet potatoes
   Roasted Sweet Potato with Rosemary 142
   Sweet Potato Casserole 147

T

Tandoori Chicken Skewers 43
Tangy Roasted Broccoli with Garlic 145
temperature conversion guide 4
temperature guide 195
Teriyaki Pork Kabobs 89
Teriyaki Wings 48
time savings 1
tomatoes
   Baked Eggs with Spinach and Tomatoes 13
   Baked Greek Omelet with Tomatoes and Feta 12
   Fish Baked with Tomatoes and Potatoes 120
   Grilled Cheese with Avocado and Tomato 36
   Sun-Dried Tomato and Goat Cheese Frittata with Basil 19
tuna
   Open-Faced Tuna Melt 33

turkey
   Herb-Roasted Turkey Breast 72
   Southwest-Style Turkey Burgers 71

V

vegetables
   Baked Parmesan Potato Wedges 159
   Baked Parmesan Zucchini Wedges 165
   Baked Potato Nachos 161
   Curried Zucchini Chips 153
   Fruit and Vegetable Skewers 158
   Greek-Style Potatoes 162
   Kale Chips 149
   Oven-Roasted Corn on the Cob 167
   Oven-Roasted Garlicky Cauliflower 169
   Roasted Balsamic Vegetables 146
   Roasted Beets and Fennel with Balsamic Glaze 157
   Roasted Carrots with Garlic and Onion 143
   Roasted Peppers 156
   Roasted Sweet Potato with Rosemary 142
   Spinach and Kale Balls with Herbs 151
   Sweet Potato Casserole 147
   Tangy Roasted Broccoli with Garlic 145
ventilation 3

W

Wasabi Salmon Burgers 127

Y

Yummy Homestyle Meatloaf 99

Z

zucchini
   Baked Parmesan Zucchini Wedges 165
   Chocolate Zucchini Bread 188
   Curried Zucchini Chips 153
   Fruit and Vegetable Skewers 158
   Lemon-Zucchini Muffins 172
   Roasted Balsamic Vegetables 146

More Bestselling Titles from Dylanna Press

Mason Jar Meals **by Dylanna Press**

Mason jar meals are a fun and practical way to take your meals on the go. Mason jars are an easy way to prepare individual servings, so whether you're cooking for one, two, or a whole crowd, these fun, make-ahead meals will work.

Includes More than 50 Recipes and Full-Color Photos

In this book, you'll find a wide variety of recipes including all kinds of salads, as well as hot meal ideas such as mini chicken pot pies and lasagna in a jar. Also included are mouth-watering desserts such as strawberry shortcake, apple pie, and s'mores.

The recipes are easy to prepare and don't require any special cooking skills. So what are you waiting for? Grab your Mason jars and start preparing these gorgeous and tasty dishes!

The Inflammation Diet by Dylanna Press

Beat Pain, Slow Aging, and Reduce Risk of Heart Disease with the Inflammation Diet

Inflammation has been called the "silent killer" and it has been linked to a wide variety of illnesses including heart disease, arthritis, diabetes, chronic pain, autoimmune disorders, and cancer.

Often, the root of chronic inflammation is in the foods we eat.

The Inflammation Diet: Complete Guide to Beating Pain and Inflammation will show you how, by making simple changes to your diet, you can greatly reduce inflammation in your body and reduce your symptoms and lower your risk of chronic disease.

The book includes a complete plan for eliminating inflammation and implementing an anti-inflammatory diet:

• Overview of inflammation and the body's immune response – what can trigger it and why chronic inflammation is harmful
• The link between diet and inflammation
• Inflammatory foods to avoid
• Anti-inflammatory foods to add to your diet to beat pain and inflammation
• Over 50 delicious inflammation diet recipes
• A 14-day meal plan

Take charge of your health and implement the inflammation diet to lose weight, slow the aging process, eliminate chronic pain, and reduce the likelihood and symptoms of chronic disease.

Learn how to heal your body from within through diet.

DASH Diet Slow Cooker Recipes **by Dylanna Press**

Delicious and Healthy DASH Diet Recipes for Your Slow Cooker

The DASH diet has once again been named the healthiest diet by top nutrition experts and there's no better time to start reaping the rewards of this smart, sensible eating plan. Eating the DASH diet way does not have to be boring, in fact, it contains the most delicious foods around – lean meats, whole grains, lots of fresh fruits and vegetables, and flavorful herbs and spices. So whether you are just starting out on the DASH diet or have been eating low-sodium for years, the *DASH Diet Slow Cooker Recipes: Easy, Delicious, and Healthy Recipes* is going to help you make delicious, healthy meals without spending a lot of time in the kitchen.

For this book, we've collected the best slow cooker recipes and adapted them to the DASH diet to create mouthwatering, family-pleasing dishes that can all be prepared easily and then cooked in your slow cooker while you're off doing other things. There's really nothing better than coming home at the end of a hectic day to the smell of tonight's dinner already prepared and waiting to be eaten.

These recipes feature fresh, whole foods and include a wide variety of recipes to appeal to every taste from classic dishes to new twists that just may become your new favorites. In addition, each recipe has less than 500 mg of sodium per serving, many a lot less than that.

In addition to recipes, the book includes a brief overview of the DASH diet as well as tips on how to get the most out of your slow cooker.

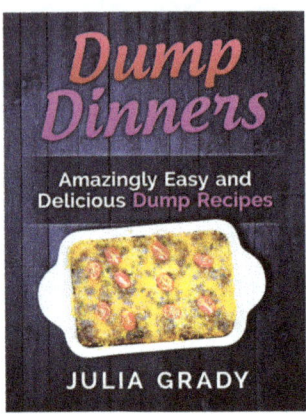

Dump Dinners: Amazingly Easy and Delicious Dump Recipes **by Julia Grady**

With the hectic pace of today's lifestyles getting dinner on the table every night is no easy task. When pressed for time, dump dinners make the perfect solution to the question, What's for dinner?

Dump dinners are so popular because they are so easy to make.

These recipes feature simple ingredients that you probably already have on hand in your freezer, refrigerator, and pantry. They do not require complicated cooking techniques or that you stand over the stove, stirring and sautéing. The majority of the recipes are mixed right in the pan they are cooked in, with the added bonus of saving cleanup time.

Delicious, Quick Recipes Your Family Will Love

This book contains the best dump dinner recipes around. None of these recipes take more than 15 minutes of hands-on time to prepare, and most a lot less. When you're short on time, you can turn to any one of these delicious recipes and have a home-cooked meal on the table with little effort and big rewards.

The recipes in this book can be cooked in several ways:
- Baked in the oven
- Cooked in a slow cooker
- Cooked on the stovetop
- Microwaved
- Frozen and cooked later

So whether you'd like to throw something in the slow cooker and come home hours later to an aromatic meal or pop a quickly prepared casserole into the oven, you are sure to find a recipe you and your family will love.

www.ingramcontent.com/pod-product-compliance
Lightning Source LLC
Chambersburg PA
CBHW081334080526
44588CB00017B/2615